Praise for *Unbroken: The Trauma Re*

"Equal parts memoir, client stories, and neuroscience, *Unbroken: The Trauma Response Is Never Wrong* will radically reframe everything you've ever thought about trauma and how to heal from it. No more feelings of shame. Just newfound empowerment."

Mark Epstein, MD
author of *Going to Pieces Without Falling Apart* and *The Zen of Therapy*

"We all experience trauma. And it leaves scars for most of us. We can learn to better handle it using Dr. MaryCatherine McDonald's fresh, positive, and scientifically rigorous approach. Her toolbox full of practical, down-to-earth advice and methods enables us to lift the burdens of shame, guilt, and fear that we all shoulder when we suffer from trauma. *Unbroken* is essential to showing us how we can become empowered, moving beyond the trauma in our past."

Allan Hamilton, MD
author of *The Scalpel and the Soul* and the
forthcoming *Cerebral Entanglements*

"I call MaryCatherine the Brené Brown of trauma. She normalizes trauma and helps us get rid of shame so that we can accept our stories fully and embrace our humanness—something that we need now in the world more than ever."

John Kim
aka The Angry Therapist

"*Unbroken* is a fascinating new book from an emerging philosophical talent."

Simon Critchley
former *New York Times* editor of The Stone column

UNBROKEN:

The Trauma Response Is Never Wrong

Also by MaryCatherine McDonald, PhD

American NATO Veteran Reintegration: The Trauma of Social Isolation and Cultural Chasms, coauthored with Gary Senecal (Lexington Books, 2021)

Merleau-Ponty and a Phenomenology of PTSD: Hidden Ghosts of Traumatic Memory (Lexington Books, 2019)

UNBROKEN:

The Trauma Response Is Never Wrong

And Other Things You
Need to Know to Take Back Your Life

MaryCatherine McDonald, PhD

sounds true
BOULDER, COLORADO

Sounds True
Boulder, CO 80306

This book is not intended as a substitute for the medical recommendations of
physicians, mental health professionals, or other health-care providers. Rather, it is
intended to offer information to help the reader cooperate with physicians, mental
health professionals, and health-care providers in a mutual quest for optimal well-
being. We advise readers to carefully review and understand the ideas presented and
to seek the advice of a qualified professional before attempting to use them.

Published 2023

Cover and book design by Charli Barnes

Printed in the United States of America

BK06361

Library of Congress Cataloging-in-Publication Data
Names: McDonald, MaryCatherine, 1981- author.
Title: Unbroken : the trauma response is never wrong : and other things you
    need to know to take back your life / MaryCatherine McDonald, PhD.
Description: Boulder, CO : Sounds True, 2023. | Includes bibliographical
    references.
Identifiers: LCCN 2022025293 (print) | LCCN 2022025294 (ebook) | ISBN
    9781683648840 (paperback) | ISBN 9781683648857 (ebook)
Subjects: LCSH: Psychic trauma--Treatment. | Traumatic neuroses.
Classification: LCC RC552.T7 M345 2023 (print) | LCC
RC552.T7 (ebook) |
    DDC 616.85/21--dc23/eng/20220923
LC record available at https://lccn.loc.gov/2022025293
LC ebook record available at https://lccn.loc.gov/2022025294

10 9 8 7 6 5 4 3 2

Hey, you.
You're not alone.

Contents

About the Stories in This Book

The client stories in this book are composites. No story is a single person's story. For protection and privacy, each story has pieces of other people's stories mixed in.

But these composites are not just about privacy, they're also about unity. If you are or have been my client and you recognize your story here, it's because it *is* your story. And it also isn't. Mine is in here too. I want you to know that even in your most isolated, lonely moment, you were not alone.

We Are Not Broken

The cure for pain is in the pain.

Rumi (translated by Coleman Barks)

Every Thursday for the better part of four years, I sat down in my therapist's office and presented him with new evidence of life's bleakness, as if I were showing him a piece of sea glass that I'd brought from a weekend at the beach.

"See? This is proof. Shards. Sharp and broken. That's all there is. It's what the sea is made of. Can't you see it?"

"Yes, I see the glass. I see the shards," he'd say. "But is that really all there is?"

To be fair, I was facing quite a lot of horror at the time. I was surrounded by tragedies, both tiny and enormous. I was twenty-five, both of my parents were suddenly dead, and what was left of my family was splintering under the weight of grief. We had sold our childhood home and my parents' thirty years' worth of belongings—and their six kids—were scattered across three states.

As time marched on, the weight of it all became too much to bear. I started to have crushing migraines, relentless panic attacks, and episodes of vertigo. Life felt like a series of nightmares. If this was what adulthood looked like, I did not want it. In a matter of months, nearly all of my most stable anchors had been pulled out of the sand and I found myself entirely at sea.

The only thing that felt stable was work. So I worked *all* the time. I collected jobs—part-time jobs, full-time jobs, classes to take, classes to teach. I nannied, was a teaching assistant, designed curricula as a contractor, and edited books. The only time I felt okay was when I could forget the circumstances of my life by losing myself in a project—preferably one with a pressing deadline. Free time meant I might have to sit with myself, and I was sure that if that happened, I would drown in my emotions, in this sea I'd discovered made of shards of glass.

Other than the distraction of work, I had exactly two coping techniques: Xanax and jumping jacks. Xanax is, theoretically, an antianxiety medication, but it has a remarkably short half-life. As soon as it wears off, panic can surge up and come bucking through your body like a downed power line. As soon as that happened, I would launch myself up from wherever I was sitting and start doing jumping jacks. My fried, frantic little brain reasoned that if I was doing jumping jacks, at least my heart would be beating fast for a *reason*, which would be a lot less scary than when it raced for *no reason*.

These coping techniques worked, sort of, but there were significant downsides. You can only take Xanax for so long, and there are many situations where breaking out into frantic jumping jacks might raise an eyebrow. What was I going to do if I had a panic attack while I was teaching? Launch into jumping jacks in the middle of a lecture? The only other option seemed to be hyperventilation.

So I didn't go to therapy just to be reminded that there was more to life than pure and abject horror. I was pretty sure there *wasn't* more to life. I went to therapy because my way of life had become unsustainable.

In one of our sessions, I sheepishly mentioned to my therapist that I had started lying on the floor when I felt terrible. I would lie on the floor in the student center, in the grad lounge, in my office, and at home. I contemplated doing it on public transportation and in the street. I was pretty sure that once I admitted this, my therapist would recommend I be committed to an institution.

Instead, he said, "That's a great grounding technique."

"A *what*?"

"A way to ground yourself. You are calming and soothing yourself by coming back to your body and feeling the stability of the floor. How cool that you reached for that without even knowing what it was! It sounds like you know exactly what you need. Maybe you should trust yourself a bit more."

Turns out, when you're feeling lost or frantic, lying on the floor provides an opposing force to the anxiety and activation. If you lie on your back and push your body into the floor, noticing and feeling each of the points where your body touches it, you start to feel mindfully aware of stability, of strength. Things start to feel more secure, and you start to feel more present. If you lie on your stomach and take some deep breaths into your belly, you activate your parasympathetic nervous system by way of the vagus nerve, which slows the heart rate and restores the body to a calm state.

I didn't know any of that at the time. I was just lying on the floor because I *needed* to. Because I was traumatized and grieving. Because I was dizzy and at sea, overwhelmed and trying to remember what land felt like. Because everything had become unbearable. *Not* because I was broken, or weak, or flawed, or doomed to suffer endlessly, but because I was strong, healthy, and aware. Even in dire straits, my poor little body and my fried, frantic little brain had *known* what they needed.

That day, something shifted. I began to see that the impulse to reach for coping strategies is a form of resilience and how that resilience is inherent within us. I began to wonder how many of us might heal if we learned more about that natural impulse to cope and how to stock our resilience toolboxes with coping strategies that work well for us.

It should be impossible to reach adulthood without a toolbox full of well-honed coping tools. Yet nearly all of us do. How did I get to age twenty-five with only *two* coping techniques: Xanax and jumping jacks? Why did I have to discover a fantastic coping exercise like lying on the floor for grounding by *accident*? Why was I ashamed of it? Why don't we teach these kinds of coping techniques in schools?

It's not because we are broken. It's because our understanding of trauma, and of our natural responses to it, is broken.

I discovered just how broken it is when I was in graduate school. At the time, not only was I learning how to cope with my own trage-dies, both tiny and enormous, but I was also looking at trauma and its effect as part of a larger question about the psychology of identity. As I went down the rabbit hole into the history of the study of trauma, I quickly found that the field of psychology is still embroiled in a war about which kinds of events count as traumatic and which do not. No wonder I had made it to age twenty-five without any coping mech-anisms! The field of psychology couldn't even get straight on what trauma *was*, let alone how people could cope with it and heal after responding to it.

What began as a study of identity became an interdisciplinary PhD dissertation on the psychology and neurobiology of the trauma response. But I didn't want everything I was learning to stay locked in the ivory tower. So alongside my dissertation, I got a life coach certification and kicked up a part-time practice. I wanted to tell as many people as I could what they were not going to learn in a traditional therapy session: That their brains and bodies were responding to overwhelm to keep them alive. That they didn't have to be ashamed of being traumatized. That the symptoms they were dealing with made sense and could be worked through. That there were tools that we could use to figure out how to counter those symptoms together. I felt compelled to help those who were struggling the way that I had.

In the past ten years, I've worked with *many* different kinds of people as a coach: military veterans; first responders; emergency room (ER) and intensive care unit (ICU) doctors; victims of sexual assault, incest, and child abuse and neglect; previously incarcerated folks; gang members; those who have lost a loved one to murder; individuals who are terminally ill; people who are chronically in pain; those trying to manage complicated grief; and people struggling after breakups, divorce, career transition, and traumatic loss. Though their stories are just about as diverse as you can imagine, what they all have in common is the desperate desire to learn how to come home to their bodies, their relationships, and the world after it has been shattered.

I have two goals for this book. The first is to undo what you think you know about trauma and replace it with what we *know* to be true after 150 years of study. As I explain in chapter 1, we have knowledge and research that shows that our previous understanding of trauma, as well as much of our understanding of trauma today, is deeply flawed. The psychological community—and thus society—used to think that the trauma response was pathology, weakness, and dysfunction. Now we *know* it is the body's natural response to threat, a sign of function and strength. In chapters 2 through 7, we'll look more closely at facets of the trauma response that are too often overlooked or misunderstood. If you have experienced traumatic events in your own life, seeing yourself in the stories of my clients will help you recognize and relate to the trauma without shame.

The second goal is to arm you with science-based coping tools that can help you wrangle what traumatic experiences leave in their wake. I want you to have a whole toolbox of coping tools, not just two. And I want you to know just how and when to use these tools. You can go and buy top-shelf tools, but if you don't know how to use them, you won't be able to build a single goddamned thing. You'll find these tools at the ends of chapters 2 through 7.

When it comes to healing after a traumatic experience and coping with the lingering symptoms of the trauma response, progress doesn't look like not having needs. It looks like learning to recognize those needs and meet them wholeheartedly. One of humanity's greatest traits is that we are malleable. We naturally adapt. What we sometimes forget is that this means we can *readapt* as well. When our coping mechanisms become unhealthy or no longer serve us, we can pick new ones. But to do so, we must be willing and ready to recognize and meet our changing needs. Only when we bring our symptoms and behaviors into the light, without shame, can we *do* something about them.

If you are struggling with the aftereffects of trauma, this book will help you drop the shame so you can understand and work with your kick-ass neurobiology—the kick-ass neurobiology that kept you alive but is now getting in your way. It will also teach you how to work with your biology's automatic responses so that you can have more sovereignty over your body and your life.

If you are trying to help someone else as they struggle with the aftereffects of trauma, this book will help you understand that person better. This will make it possible for you to anticipate their trauma responses, not personalize them, and help your person navigate more sustainable, connected coping.

No matter who you are, I hope that above all you will come away with the understanding that trauma does not equal brokenness. That's a myth, a fallacy. The idea that traumatic experience breaks us is based on shame and bad science. What our traumatic experiences reveal is that though we can be bent, dented, or bruised, we *cannot* be broken. That, in fact, we are the *unbroken*.

CHAPTER 1

Repairing Our Understanding of Trauma
Trading Shame for Science

No trauma has discrete edges. Trauma bleeds. Out
of wounds and across boundaries.

Leslie Jamison

F orget everything you think you know about trauma. Most of it comes from outdated definitions, poor societal understanding, and science that has since been overturned by new technology. Too often we think of trauma in terms of what happened—like an attack, a natural disaster, a serious accident or illness, a war, or a loss.

What if, instead, we thought about trauma in terms of the *reaction* an experience causes?

Something is potentially traumatic when it overwhelms the nervous system enough to cause our emergency coping mechanisms to kick into gear. These mechanisms are designed to save our lives—and they do. But to do so, they pull energy and resources from some of our other systems, including those that help us orient ourselves in the world and organize our memories.

Most of the time, when our emergency mechanisms activate, they get toggled back off pretty quickly and our nervous system regains normal function. Sometimes, though, we have trouble finding the off switch, and the emergency system stays on. Chronically activated emergency systems trick us into thinking we are constantly in danger, and what was an isolated incident becomes a never-ending feedback loop. Our nervous system starts to perceive nearly everything as danger, which radically changes how we feel in our bodies and in the world.

When this happens, we need someone to help us retrain our system to toggle back off by providing a safe haven for us to process and feel. When this relational process cannot (or simply does not) happen, what was potentially traumatic becomes a *lasting trauma*.

Sounds simple and logical enough, right? To keep a potentially traumatic experience from becoming lasting trauma, we just need to find someone (or more than one person) to help us cope in the short term and reset our system in the long term. So what keeps that from happening?

There could be many things affecting each of us individually, but as a trauma researcher, I can point to one big reason that affects all of us: shame.

We have been fed a great societal lie that says continuing to suffer after experiencing a traumatic event is something we should be ashamed of. We are told that suffering after trauma is something that should be kept to oneself. It is, after all, a sign of weakness, proof of a great and intractable character flaw. There is the trauma, and then there is the way you respond to the trauma, and if you do not respond with the kind of automatic, effortless, and sparkling resilience that makes other people feel comfortable, then you have failed. You *are* a failure.

Unfortunately, this lie is a long-standing one, and it is rooted in how the study of trauma has developed throughout the history of clinical psychology.

THE HISTORY OF THE STUDY OF TRAUMA

The history of the study of trauma can be divided into five phases, one of which we are in now. I promise not to bore you with unnecessary historical detail, but a few key moments reflect how we understand and view trauma today in some important ways. Looking at what we know about the study of trauma so far, we can see how it has shaped our current understanding in harmful ways. That knowledge is critical as we assess and update our current understanding of trauma.

Phase One

The first phase took place in ancient Egypt, where depressive symptoms coupled with baffling physical episodes in women were termed "hysteria" and believed to be the result of a "wandering uterus." Curative methods were designed to "move" the uterus back to where it belonged. Hippocrates, who you may know as the father of the practice of medicine and the namesake of the Hippocratic oath, believed that hysterical symptoms such as anxiety, tremors, convulsions, and paralysis could be traced to sexual inactivity. The cure, accordingly, was sexual activity, which was thought to restore women and their uteruses to their proper function.

Though this might seem absurd, it's worth remembering that in the absence of modern medical technology, diagnostics and treatments in the ancient world were based almost entirely in hypothesis. Further, though the idea about the origins of hysteria turned out to be wrong, ancient Egyptians were right about many other things. Even without modern technology, they successfully treated bone breaks, dental issues, and many other aches, pains, and diseases.

Later cultures argued about whether abstinence or more sexual activity was the better cure, but the idea that the cluster of symptoms originated in the dysfunction of female reproductive organs remained unchanged for a long time.

The psychiatric community consistently failed to find a sustainable, successful treatment for hysteria. It became regarded as the mental illness most difficult to treat, and women who suffered from it were relegated to insane asylums and subjected to either neglect or torturous experimental methods.

Phase Two

The second critical phase in the history of the study of trauma took place in western Europe in the late 1800s when a group of influential psychologists became taken with the unsolvable problem of the hysterical woman. Jean-Martin Charcot, Sigmund Freud, Josef Breuer, and Pierre Janet all found themselves spending most of their time with their hysterical patients, and together they made some of the first strides in understanding what was going on with them.

In the mid-1860s, Charcot brought attention to the problem with his famed "Tuesday night lectures." These lectures drew crowds who came to watch hysterical women "perform" their symptoms on stage.

In 1895, when Freud and Breuer published their work *Studies on Hysteria*, they theorized that the cause of hysteria was past trauma. Though Freud and Breuer are complicated figures in the history of psychology, the breakthroughs they made in their study of trauma still shape the way that we understand it today. Completely by accident, Freud and Breuer discovered that their patients' untreatable symptoms could always be traced back to a precipitating event that was too emotionally overwhelming to process in the moment. They theorized that an inability to process an upsetting event because of an extreme emotional response caused that event to get stuck in the psyche somehow and cause chronic symptoms. They hoped that if they could help their patients process the initial event and bear some of the unbearable emotions, the symptoms would cease. We may take this idea for granted now, but at the time, the theory that some kind of event could explode the recording and processing system in the brain and lead to chronic mental health issues was a radical one.

Janet came to the same conclusion while working separately from Freud and Breuer. He was the first to connect the theory of dissociation to traumatic memories. This connection explained why hysterical patients often experienced an altered state of consciousness that made them feel as though they had "left the room." Like Freud and Breuer, Janet speculated that intense emotions have an effect on the mind's ability to process an event and led the mind to create a different kind of memory, one that is somatic (bodied), rather than cognitive (mental), and manifests in dreams, hyper-aroused states, and flashbacks.

Had the history of the study of trauma continued to proceed as fruitfully as it began in the late 1800s, there is no telling how far it might have progressed by now. Unfortunately, it came to a screeching halt almost as soon as it had begun.

Charcot's work began to face scrutiny when it was suggested that the subjects of his Tuesday night lectures were acting rather than experiencing true hysterical symptoms. Janet and Freud became entangled in a feud when Janet accused Freud of plagiarizing his work on hysteria. In response, Janet shifted his focus to developing a more comprehensive theory of the mind. Meanwhile, Freud and Breuer abandoned their patients mid-treatment and repudiated their own work—not because their theory was wrong, but because it was right. They started to realize that all their patients were facing trauma from the same traumatic stressor: sexual abuse. The problem was, many of their patients were the daughters of close friends who were esteemed members of society. Having to grapple with what appeared to be an epidemic of sexual assault among their peers and betters was something Freud and Breuer were not prepared to take on. It was far easier to abandon their theory and their patients than to defend them.

But Freud and Breuer did not abandon their method. Some of the central ideas in *Studies on Hysteria*—the "talking cure" being the most notable example—remain mainstays of their later work and of psychoanalytic theory and practice today.

While Charcot, Freud, Breuer, and Janet came to understand that hysteria may not originate in the uterus or be related to a lack of or an excess of sexual activity, it was still seen as a disorder that exclusively afflicted women. Thus, it was during this phase that the word *trauma* first became entangled with the words *weakness* or *dysfunction* and the notions those words carry with them. To become traumatized was to be weak and feminine, a victim. As we will see, the idea that trauma only affects women and weak men is socially problematic and stigmatizing. And the idea that trauma is a sign of weakness is scientifically and neurobiologically just plain wrong.

Phase Three

The third critical phase occurred when the field of psychology finally had to accept that trauma impacted men as well as women. This happened after World War I, when soldiers returning home began displaying symptoms of hysteria despite their incontestable lack of a uterus. Plagued by bouts of altered consciousness, emotional outbursts, paralysis, amnesia, and muteness, these soldiers forced the discussion of these symptoms back into the psychological landscape. There were just too many suffering soldiers to ignore.

At first, the theory was that these symptoms were still physiologically based, just not in the uterus. This time, the hypothesis was that repetitive exposure to exploding shells caused concussions, which in turn resulted in a kind of brain damage. This is where the term *shell shock* came from: concussive blasts equal concussions equal shell shock.

This theory was quickly abandoned because many of the soldiers with shell shock had *not* been exposed to exploding shells. Without a clear physiological cause of the symptoms, and without any way of understanding why some came back from war altered and others did not, blame was shifted onto the *character* of the suffering soldier.

To suffer from shell shock was to fail. And this failure was gendered; to have an emotional response to combat meant that a soldier had failed as a man. It meant he was frail, broken, weak, guilty, inadequate, and lesser than—all qualities associated with being female and hysterical. To succeed as a soldier was either to evade this fate altogether (the best option), or to heal by getting rid of these feminine evils and returning to the original and true masculine strength. This bias led to treatments that used humiliation and violence to snap soldiers out of their altered "feminine" states and turn them back into heroic men.

While being traumatized no longer meant someone had a wandering uterus, in too many circles it still meant someone was weak. Like the first phase in the study of trauma, this one waned when the psychological theory failed to capture the complexity of the symptoms.

Phase Four

The fourth pivotal phase in the history of the study of trauma occurred nearly one hundred years after Freud and company. This phase began when the psychological community finally realized that the hysteria that plagued women and the war trauma that plagued soldiers were the same beast. This new understanding came about because of two things that happened independently yet simultaneously. First, after the Vietnam War researchers once again began looking closely at postwar trauma in veterans. (Spikes in the study of trauma have happened with each war since World War I.) Second, the study of sexual assault, sexual harassment, and domestic violence also increased in the 1970s, '80s, and '90s. Clinicians finally realized that traumatic experience was not gendered and could impact the psychology of *anyone*. In other words, the cluster of symptoms was not unique to women or to soldiers. At last, the term *post-traumatic stress* (PTS) was added to the *Diagnostic and Statistical Manual of Mental Disorders*, third edition (DSM-III), clinical psychology's encyclopedia of mental disorders, in 1980.

This phase came to a halt in the early 1990s, when a series of studies suggested that therapists were planting false trauma memories in the minds of their clients. The suspicion cast on the entire field of trauma studies was so intense that in 2009, when I chose trauma as my area of PhD research, my professors warned me against studying something that had been proven to be fake.

The Recurring Pattern

In each of these four phases we can see an oscillating pattern: there is a looking toward trauma, an intense study, a new kind of legitimacy, and then an abrupt turning away. This pattern has been both noticed and lamented by many important figures in the history of the study of trauma. Abram Kardiner and Herbert Spiegel, pioneers in trauma theory after World War II, lamented that trauma is "not subject to continuous study, . . . but only to periodic efforts which cannot be characterized as very diligent."[1] Judith Herman, a feminist trauma theorist, calls the study of trauma one of "episodic amnesia."[2] Veteran and war journalist David Morris calls the world of trauma studies "remarkably chaotic," resembling "an arcade at a state fair . . . with little overlap between various groups, let alone coherence."[3]

It is not that the study of trauma falls out of favor due to a lack of interest, or that there are periods of time in which trauma does not occur, but, as Herman says, "the subject provokes such intense contro-versy that it periodically becomes anathema."[4] The word *anathema* has its roots in the Greek words for "an object representing destruction." The study itself seems to become a kind of destructive force, threat-ening things we believe about ourselves, about society, or about the way human beings experience the world. We turn toward the study of trauma until doing so forces us to come to grips with uncomfortable aspects of ourselves and our world, and then we turn away. And each time that we turn our backs on the examination of traumatic experi-ence, we relegate those who suffer from it to the recesses of the insane asylum—literally, figuratively, or both.

WHERE WE ARE TODAY

I would argue that we are currently living through the fifth pivotal phase in the study of trauma. The advent of brain imaging technology, which allows us to see blood flow into different structures of the brain in dif-ferent circumstances, means we can no longer ignore how overwhelming experiences leave their mark on our nervous system. Plus, a constellation of events—political strife, the coronavirus pandemic, and a marked increase in public discussion of mental illness—has brought the idea of trauma once again to the forefront of our collective consciousness. We are talking about trauma much more than we used to. This is a good thing for many reasons. It means we are starting to see that trauma is, in fact, real and legitimate, which makes it even more likely that people who need help will be able to get it. However, the current agreed upon clinical definition hasn't caught up with all the progress we've made in neuroscience and psychology so far in this phase. This is a huge, huge problem, because our societal understanding of trauma comes from the field of clinical psychology.

Anyone who googles *trauma* or *PTSD* (post-traumatic stress disor-der) will get definitions from the DSM, which is now in its fifth edition (DSM-V). These definitions shape the way we view and talk about trauma.

The DSM is jokingly called the "clinical bible" because everyone uses it as a reference and because, much like the actual Bible, the interpretation of its contents is the topic of debate. Sometimes these debates are so intense that they create factions among clinical sects, keeping everyone from getting any work done.

The original intent of the DSM was to serve as a reference guide for clinicians and researchers so they could track data and take note of trends. Is major depressive disorder more common in areas of socio-economic decline? Does the onset of schizophrenia seem to happen at a certain age? How often is generalized anxiety disorder comorbid with substance use disorder?

The reason that the DSM gained such a stronghold is because the taxonomy of mental disorders made it easy for medical insurance companies to decide who to cover and for how long. For example, a biologically based mental illness—one that is rooted in your biology, like bipolar disorder or schizophrenia—is something that the insurance company could liken to a physical illness and cover accordingly. On the other hand, a personality disorder, which is currently thought to occur largely because of your environment rather than your biology, would be covered differently (or not at all).

The DSM gets revised every handful of years to account for advancements in research. This means the diagnostic categories therein are somewhat of a moving target, which only adds to the complex nature of diagnostics.

The DSM is widely available but not discussed enough to be widely understood or properly contextualized. The fact that much of the DSM is available for free on the internet is a mixed blessing. Mental health resources can be difficult and expensive to access. And yet, what we do with that access matters. We might be tempted to diagnose ourselves and each other using a tool that is imperfect at best and that we have not been trained to use. Clinical language can be co-opted to support social trends. You might notice, for example, that suddenly everyone your best friend has ever dated is a "narcissist" or all your mother's neighbors are "socio-paths." The DSM in untrained hands can be as dangerous as a chainsaw.

While having knowledge about prevalent character traits and mental disorders can be an important starting point for understanding your-self and those around you, it is hardly exhaustive. To use a gardening metaphor, in order to grow a thriving garden, you can begin with packets of seeds, but you also need to know how much water and sunlight they need. Simply guess and you run the risk of killing your poor plants before they even have a chance to grow roots.

The other thing that the DSM does not contain is any historical information about the way that diagnostic clusters evolve over time and why. This history is especially important when it comes to the definition of trauma because the definition we have all been using is mostly wrong and has become deeply harmful, both clinically and societally.

The current DSM entry for PTSD specifies that to be diagnosed, a patient must have had exposure to a traumatic stressor. On the face of it, this makes sense. If someone hasn't gone through a trauma, the odds of them developing a disorder related to trauma are pretty slim. However, this version of the DSM does not simply say that one must have experienced a trauma, it specifies three things that *count* as traumatic: actual or threatened death, actual or threatened serious injury, and actual or threatened sexual violence.

Three things. There are just *three things* that count as potentially traumatic.

You might think this is not really a problem because this is only the view of the world of clinical psychology. You would be wrong for two reasons.

First, it *is* a problem even within clinical psychology. If you are suffering from a trauma that does not fit within these criteria and you have a clinician who takes the DSM definition literally (as many, but not all, do), you will be diagnosed and treated for something other than trauma. That treatment might have a beneficial effect in the way that an improvised tourniquet might save your limb or life temporarily.

Second, these clinical categories are a problem because they do not stay siloed in the clinical world. Clinical debates and opinions get filtered into society through the media in more ways than can possibly be accounted for. They infiltrate the way we all regard and speak about trauma. Plus, even if you have never seen PTSD or trauma mentioned on the news or any social media platform, the DSM with this set of criteria—this list of three things that can potentially be traumatic—is the very first thing that comes up when you type "PTSD" into Google.

And these are only the most direct ways we can see the overlap between the world of clinical psychology and society at large.

The reason the list hasn't been expanded further is because of a very real and very valid concern: if we expand the definition too broadly, we risk stretching the word *trauma* to meaninglessness. If *anything* can potentially be traumatizing, then trauma simply becomes a trivial aspect of human life, no longer worthy of any research or study. This is a real risk.

I once overheard a woman at Starbucks lament that the store had sold out of pumpkin spice syrup and that this was (insert a Valley girl accent) "deeply *traumatic*." My students have told me, while smirking, that they have been "traumatized" both by chemistry exams and bad cafeteria food. Once, after hearing that I study trauma for a living, a man at a party regaled me with a story about how his wife neglected to call him by his pet name while trying to get his attention in a dangerous situation, and he had retaliated with four days of silent treatment. He clearly wanted my approval. Wide-eyed and dripping with counterfeit vulnerability, he explained, "It's, like, she *forgot* that I really *prefer* my pet name, you know? That's some *trauma* right there, isn't it?"

Probably not, *Pumpkin*.

Bending and stretching the language of trauma to meet our desires—to seem legitimate, to account for our bad behavior, to hide behind—is not helpful. We need to find a definition that accounts for the many things that can potentially be traumatic without running the risk of becoming watered down into meaninglessness.

How do we do that? I have an idea, and we'll return to it in chapter 8. But here's what you need to know right now: Even though there's debate in clinical psychology about the clinical definition of trauma, there's no debate within your body, mind, and emotions. If you're in a trauma response, it means something traumatic has happened to you—regardless of what the DSM, clinicians, insurance companies, or society says. Your body, mind, and emotions are saying there's something you need to attend to. What we've missed (and what the history of the study of trauma has obscured in some sense) is this fact that the trauma response system is a necessary part of our biology.

THE NEUROBIOLOGY OF THE TRAUMA RESPONSE: A PRIMER

One of the things that makes the experience of trauma so lasting, so devastating, and so disruptive is the misappropriation of shame to the traces that trauma leaves in its wake. This idea that suffering after trauma is shameful rests on a foundation of bad science and the resulting belief that emotions are separate from biology. They are not. One of the gifts the fifth phase in the history of the study of trauma offers is the recognition that emotions are biological events and the constellation of symptoms that make up PTSD are as real and as rooted in the body as a broken bone.

Each of the stories in chapters 2 through 7 will explain how the trauma response works in our biology, so I want to start with a primer on the brain. My goal is to give you a layperson's understanding of *some* of the things at play to illustrate that traumatic experiences impact our brains and bodies.

It is worth noting that neuroscience is an incredibly complex and fast-paced field of study and that research is shifting daily. What I unpack here does not capture the full extent of what we know or the kinds of debates that exist around some of these concepts. So if you happen to be a neuroscientist, just know that I know how much more complicated all of this is, and maybe just skip ahead to chapter 2.

To understand the trauma response, there are five parts of the brain and body we need to get to know.

The prefrontal cortex

The amygdala

The hippocampus

The hypothalamus

The sympathetic and parasympathetic nervous systems

I like to think of the prefrontal cortex as the executive assistant of my brain. I imagine Pepper Potts from *Ironman*—rational and quick-witted, often saving the day with a measured and careful response to more impulsive and sometimes ill-conceived thoughts and ideas. The prefrontal cortex lies in the very front of the brain, behind the eyes. It is highly intelligent and organized. It oversees things like rational thought, decision making, working memory (memory that is required to complete tasks in the moment, like making a dish from a cookbook), and language recognition and processing. Neural connections to this part of the brain develop last, so babies and toddlers do not have very well-established access to it.

The amygdala is nestled in the center of the brain and is a little bigger than a walnut. It is critical in the regulation of emotions, emotional behavior, and motivations. While the neurobiology of emotions is a good deal more complicated than we can go into here, it is most important for us to understand that the amygdala registers fear and threat. When animals or human beings do not have access to the amygdala, they cannot feel fear. You can think of it like a smoke alarm on the ceiling of your kitchen. Its chief job is to alert you when you are in danger. This part of the brain develops early and is not very sophisticated. The amygdala simply registers a threat, and if the prefrontal cortex is online, these two parts of the brain together can decide whether the threat is actual or perceived.

The hippocampus is nestled toward the back of the brain and is necessary in the formation and long-term storage of memories. Learning and memory are impossible without it. I like to think of the hippocampus as a filing room. It has neatly organized file cabinets that order our long-term memories into folders. Each memory folder has three components: a narrative of the event, emotional content pertaining to it, and a set of meanings (chronological, personal, emotional). This filing system makes it possible to reach for memories, talk about them and feel some of the emotional content, and then put them away with relative ease.

The hypothalamus is directly over the brain stem and oversees sending messages between the brain and the body through the autonomic nervous system (ANS). You can think of the ANS as a marionette and the hypothalamus as the puppeteer who pulls the strings. These strings are connected to all the involuntary functions in your body, such as heart rate, digestion, breathing rate, and blood pressure. The functioning of the hypothalamus is complex, but the main thing to understand about it is this: its job is to keep you alive by altering how you function in the presence or absence of threat.

To really understand what the hypothalamus is doing, we need to look at a small part of the nervous system. You can think of the nervous system as a control panel that helps the different systems and parts of your body communicate. The ANS is the part of the control panel that is responsible for the functioning of your internal organs. It up- or downregulates your blood pressure, heart rate, and other involuntary processes by toggling between the sympathetic and parasympathetic branches, which are turned on and off by the hypothalamus. In the presence of a threat, the hypothalamus flips a switch and the sympathetic nervous system activates, increasing our blood pressure, heart rate, and breathing rate, among other things. When the threat subsides, the hypothalamus flips the switch back and the parasympathetic nervous system slows everything down—our blood pressure drops, our heart rate comes down, and our breathing slows.

If your brain were a video game, its goal would be homeostasis. This just means there would be equal blood flow and electrical activity throughout the cortex (the outer layer of the brain with all those creepy looking gray folds). When this happens, all systems are online and getting the right amount of energy to function well. The brain is constantly taking in data from the world outside and from inside the body, regulating blood flow and electrical activity accordingly. When an overwhelming event happens, your brain goes through a set of automatic responses to make sure that you stay alive. It kicks on the mechanisms of fight, flight, or freeze to help you survive in moments of extreme stress and danger. When you are pushed into a corner but feel like you can take on the enemy, you fight. When you are being chased by something you cannot fight, you flee. When you are stuck in a situation where you can neither fight nor flee, you freeze.

These mechanisms are evolutionary and biological. They are our parachutes. They are rooted in our will to *survive*, to cope, and to adapt to a world that we do not always have control over. These mechanisms also are sometimes hard to regain control over and can create lasting and crippling symptoms. But all of them are designed to *save* us in the moment of overwhelm. When we understand that, we can see how attaching shame to the trauma response is unwarranted and unhelpful.

LETTING GO OF SHAME

Understanding the basic biological script that begins when a traumatic event happens *and* continues when a traumatic event is remembered is critical for healing. It is much harder to feel toxic shame for something that is rooted in your biology. If you got a migraine in the middle of a date, you might feel *really* irritated, inconvenienced, and embarrassed even. You might wonder if showing your bodily vulnerability too early will make your date decide you are too high maintenance to go out with again. None of this is pleasant, but it's also not soul crushing. At some point, even amidst all the worry, you would come to understand that migraines are simply a part of your neurobiology.

The way that we absorb and respond to overwhelming traumatic events is also a part of our neurobiology—not a flaw in it. The fact that we can respond to the overwhelm of traumatic events in the way that we do is miraculous, lifesaving, and proof of strength and adaptability, not a sign of weakness.

Please remember this. It's important. *The trauma response is rooted in strength, not weakness.*

The trauma response keeps us alive. Without it we would not exist. It is rooted in strength and the human drive to survive. So when we shame ourselves and others for suffering because of it, we are shaming ourselves for being human. Trauma has become entangled with shame, and shame, being both metastatic *and* highly contagious, must be avoided at all costs. So instead of teaching people how to cope with traumatic experiences, we pretend that it is possible to avoid them or to sail through them unscathed. We do not teach coping strategies because we view mental health as the norm and mental illness as the aberration—as if our response to a traumatic experience is a kind of moral failing. That shame only makes it that much harder to address the aftereffects of the trauma response, which admittedly can be challenging. We are getting in our own way, over and over and over again.

If we can digest just a little of the neurobiology of our trauma response, we can combat some of this shame, as individuals and as a society. We can counter the great societal lie that says experiencing a trauma response long after an overwhelming event is a sign of weakness, failure, or dysfunction. This is imperative because our broken understanding of trauma isn't just bad science; it is preventing people from healing.

CHAPTER 2

Malcolm's Fight Club
When Trauma Upends Our View of the World

Stories are for joining the past to the future. Stories are for those late
hours in the night when you can't remember how you got from where
you were to where you are. Stories are for eternity, when memory
is erased, when there is nothing to remember except the story.

Tim O'Brien

The lighting in Malcolm's bedroom is so dim that it feels a bit
like I'm interviewing someone in a witness protection program.
During our video call, he asks me three or four times whether
this session is *really* confidential. Then he checks again by email about
a week later.

Malcolm's speech pattern is jagged and fast as he explains he's come
to me because he heard I might be able to help him heal from combat
trauma. He reassures me that he's good, that he's really fine, that he has
it completely under control. It really hasn't been an issue at all. But his
wife has just left and she has a different take on the whole thing.

I start to wonder if these reassurances are for him or for me, as each
one of them starts to unravel as soon as the words leave his mouth.

Malcolm survived several deployments during the long wars in Iraq
and Afghanistan. But now his military career is over, and there are some

lasting effects from his experience. Within twenty minutes or so, he has rattled off a list of things he's seen and been through that would make your stomach lurch. I can feel him getting more amped as the minutes spin by. The list is punctuated by more frantic assurances that he really isn't struggling anymore. He's stopped having those nightmares. He only marches the perimeter of his house at night. He no longer plans to kill himself. "This is better. Right? I'm fine. Right? I'm fine. It's fine. What were we talking about?"

I think the reassurances are for both of us. What Malcolm is dealing with feels bigger than the two of us, bigger than any of us. What has been revealed to him at war are a series of essential truths about life and human existence that most of us spend our whole lives trying not to think about: Life is terrifying. We are vulnerable. Our moral structures are human made, not inherent. And they sometimes crumble.

Malcolm tells me that he became closer to people in his battalion than he'd thought possible. And then he watched them die, often in ways that would make Quentin Tarantino look away. The fact that he survived doesn't make sense to him. Sure, he's a good guy. But they were good guys too. They were all "doing the right thing in a tough spot," he keeps saying. Most people don't know what it's like "doing the right thing in a tough spot." It's the only sentence he utters that truly sounds like his own. The rest of his words sound borrowed, threadbare.

Malcolm had struggled with many of the things you might expect: traumatic flashbacks that sometimes left him raging at family members, bouts of drinking so intense he couldn't remember entire months at a time, and a hypervigilance that made it impossible to sit still or to sleep. Once he ripped part of his white picket fence out of the ground with his hands in the middle of the night because it seemed ridiculous to him. It wasn't protective enough. "Fucking white picket fence," he says. "Can you believe it? Goddamn American dream. *Fuck*."

Though some of this was certainly heartbreaking, none of it was a dealbreaker for his wife. The thing she was drawing the line at was the fight club. Malcolm could not, would not, give it up. And she could not keep tending to the new wounds that he swore were healing him.

If you thought of that movie with Brad Pitt and Edward Norton when you got to the phrase "fight club," you went to the right place. A couple of nights a week, Malcolm and a group of grown men, mostly combat vets, met in an undisclosed location and fought until someone fell unconscious. Malcolm was beating himself up. (Well, other people were beating him up, but they were doing so at his request.) He had come home, but he was still very much at war—with himself, with his wife, and with strangers. Malcolm was traumatized. And he was morally injured.

TRAUMA AS MORAL INJURY

After the Vietnam War, clinicians started to notice that they had missed part of what it means to have trauma after war. Not only was the experience of war—of both seeing and participating in atrocities— overwhelming, but the experience of survival could be as well. So in 1980, the American Psychological Association added a clause to DSM's entry for PTSD. The clause specified that symptoms of trauma might include "guilt about surviving while others have not, or about behavior required for survival."[1] The clause disappeared in the next rewrite of the DSM, and so to replace it, clinicians have started using the term *moral injury*.

The idea behind moral injury is that a key part of trauma is the experience of being haunted either by the sense that *you* have failed morally or that your moral structures have failed *you*.

This second meaning—the idea that your moral structures have failed you—applies to any kind of traumatic experience. In fact, this is a central part of trauma's wound. Think of it this way: Regardless of your spiritual life and beliefs, all of us have a set of assumptions about the way the world works. These assumptions stretch from the mundane to the meaningful, and they help us order and navigate the world so that it feels less chaotic. They are a part of our map of the world. For example: Tuesday comes after Monday. In the United States, income taxes are due April 15. Smoking is bad for you. Bad things only happen to bad people. Everyone gets what they are owed in life. We will all ultimately meet our demise.

You also operate under a set of assumptions that conform to the circumstances of your *particular* life. The dog will always barf on the carpet and not the tile. The trash collectors will come on Thursday morning and make far too much noise for 5:45 a.m. Your youngest child will always be quirky. When your spouse leaves the house for work in the morning, they will return by dinner.

These little beliefs and assumptions are signposts in our map of the world. We start drawing that map the day we are born, and we refine it as we go. When we learn something important—kittens can scratch you, fire burns—we put a signpost on the map. When we've got enough of a map and enough signposts to navigate through the world, we frame our map and put it on the wall. When we're feeling lost, confused, or at sea, the map and the signposts we've placed on it orient us and make us feel grounded and in control. Each time the world conforms to our expectations, we are reassured. We've put the signposts in the right places.

But when the world does not conform to our expectations, we have a problem. One day, our spouse leaves for work and *doesn't* return by dinner—doesn't return at all, in fact. And our beautifully framed, accurately drawn map comes crashing from the wall and shatters to pieces on the living room floor. We are forced to cope with the loss *and* our shattered map.

This shattering is moral injury. When the very structures of morality crumble in the face of traumatic experience, the world stops making sense *altogether*. It's not just one belief, one specific signpost, that's iffy—it's the whole damn map. How are you supposed to move forward when the world teaches you that bad things *don't* only happen to bad people? Though we might operate from our map unconsciously for the most part, when these signposts crumble, their role in our lives becomes staggeringly clear. They guide us; we depend on them. Without them, we are lost. When they disappear, we are forced to reevaluate them and create new ones. And trauma often reveals that most of them are made-up. They are fictions—necessary ones that help us navigate the world, but fictions nonetheless.

When Malcolm unflinchingly told me about the fight club, I remember being absolutely stopped in my tracks. I wanted to make sure the shock didn't register on my face. I also wanted to make sure that I could help him see what he was doing and why, and why the fight club was so heartbreaking for his wife. Perhaps the problem was not that she didn't understand, but that she did. I wanted to help him find another way to get his adrenaline out or another way to lay his shame to rest—or both.

From a clinical perspective, there are three central features to moral injury. First, there is self-blame. In Malcolm's case, he blamed himself for having survived. Though there was no evidence he had failed any of his fellow soldiers, he found himself wondering sometimes. Beating himself up was a way of absolving himself, as a way of making sense of his own survival. If he survived but was constantly bruised, bloodied, and in pain, perhaps the scales evened out a little.

The second clinical feature of moral injury is an inability to trust either oneself or other people. Researchers have discovered that when events involve personal responsibility, the lack of trust is directed at oneself. When events involve other people and their failure to take responsibility (or their betrayal of their responsibility), the lack of trust is directed at other people. Malcolm didn't trust himself. There is an incredible burden that comes with senseless survival. If I survived and they didn't, does that mean I'm here for some special reason? If so, how do I find out what that is and make sure I live up to it? Don't I owe them at least that? Malcolm couldn't trust himself, so he punished himself. Only instead of wearing sackcloth and ashes, Malcolm chose to get his head kicked in every Wednesday night.

The third clinical feature of moral injury is spiritual/existential crisis. This feature is perhaps the most fatal. When the seams of the world start to burst and everything stops making sense all at the same time, how can you possibly go on? If none of the structures of meaning you previously believed in stand true, everything becomes meaningless. If everything is meaningless, why bother? Not only did being in physical pain restore some sense of order in the world, some cause and effect, but it also brought Malcolm a little closer to death. There was something comforting in that. Part of him clearly felt he should be dead.

THE HUMILIATION OF MORAL INJURY

There is a fourth feature to moral injury that does not appear in the clinical understanding: humiliation. It can feel humiliating to learn the world does not operate the way you thought it did, that your beliefs about how the world works were not accurate in the first place. Shouldn't you have noticed your flawed outlook sooner? Shouldn't you have seen this coming? It's a little bit like rushing around the kitchen and accidentally dropping and shattering your favorite mug in your haste. Your face instantly flushes with frustration and regret. You should have seen that coming; you should have been more careful.

Only in this case, Malcolm doesn't understand why he wasn't the mug.

It was not just that Malcolm felt guilty for having survived the war when others didn't, it was that he could not figure out *why*. If good things happen to good people, why did his fellow soldiers—who were "the best kind of good"—die? Malcolm was not just facing the guilt or shame that comes from an act one has done (or failed to do, or that someone else has done). His experience at war had thrown the meaning of the world in general into question. Malcolm was beating himself up because the world didn't make sense, and therefore it was unbearable. He was also beating himself up because he felt like he deserved it. Not just because he lived and his friends didn't, but because his map of the world had gotten ripped away, and he didn't see it coming. He should have known. It was *fucking humiliating*.

When our structures of meaning and morality crumble, we feel humiliated for having counted on them in the first place. This is one of the reasons that shame and trauma are so entangled. We are *ashamed* for having counted on something, for having believed a pretty little lie about the world. Shame on us for having so blithely counted on our stupid maps and silly signposts.

Imagine drawing a map of the town you live in, and then tracing a path from your house to the grocery store. You have only your life experience to pull from, but you confidently trace the path, having taken that route to the store hundreds of times. Now imagine you tried to get to the grocery store using only your confidently drawn map, and you ended up lost in the forest instead of at the store. Who would you blame?

Tell a veteran, or a victim of sexual assault or child abuse, or someone who has just suffered a traumatic loss, that what happened was not their fault, and they will either wave you away or simply sit there blinking. It is not because they don't believe you, it is because you've missed the point. Part of what gets revealed in the experience of trauma is a paradox about being human: we *cannot* predict what will happen, and we simultaneously *must* predict what will happen in order to function. What a traumatic experience reveals is that though there might be some rules to the universe and some things we might be able to count on, these rules are mostly created by us. They aren't infallible. We draw our own maps, and sometimes they are wrong. They aren't to existential scale.

The truth is, sometimes we hold on to shame and blame because the alternative is *so much worse*. If you are sexually assaulted and believe you are to blame for what happened, you also believe that preventing future assault is in your control. If it was your fault, you can prevent it in the future. If it is not your fault, then you have to accept that to be human is to be vulnerable to harm. If it is not your fault, the signpost that reads "bad things only happen to bad people" has to be replaced with one that reads, "there is senseless evil in the world." Given the option of two painful pills, one will likely choose the least painful one to swallow. Shame, though corrosive, is containable. The lesson that life is terrifying is not.

Malcolm participated in the fight club because he had no outlet for his adrenaline and because he felt like he deserved the pain and humiliation both for what he did and didn't do in combat. But he also participated in the fight club because he thought that if he entered the battle on purpose, it couldn't catch him unawares. He was trying to anticipate and manage future humiliation because he hadn't been able to in the past.

Slowly, Malcolm started to unpack all of this and really heal. He moved into a condo without a white picket fence. His wife didn't come back, but they're good friends. He feels like she understands a part of him that nobody else could. In a way, she did the right thing in a tough spot. He has a new girlfriend.

Most importantly, he gave up the fight club. For our last session, he called from his car on the way to a jiujitsu class. We had been trying to come up with some coping techniques to replace his dangerous ones, and he'd come up with jiujitsu. It worked. Because here's the thing: The idea that life is meaningless is only *half* the story. It's not meaningless full stop—it's meaningless *except* for the meaning that we assign it. The fact that there are no inherent truths or moral structures in the world can actually be empowering and not destructive. If the rules are not inherent, that means we get to stop searching for them and make our own.

Just because your map falls off the wall and shatters to pieces doesn't mean you are doomed to wander and suffer for the rest of your life. It just means you have to draw another map.

TAKEAWAYS AND TOOLS

You'll remember from chapter 1 that Freud and Breuer discovered what they called "the talking cure" entirely by accident when they were working with traumatized patients. They found that talking about events—now known as *narrating*—made it possible for patients to rethink them and put them away. While we have many new interventions for healing trauma, the talking cure has been a mainstay undergirding psychotherapy in general.

Narrative therapy is a method where the patient and therapist or coach work together to develop a rich and vivid account of the life story of the patient, focusing on significant events.

Narrative is a powerful tool because of the way that human psychology is structured. We organize and understand our lives by rendering them into story form. These stories then make up the fabric of personal consciousness. They help us understand the world and our roles within it. In other words, it is not just what has happened to us that is relevant, but also the stories we tell to ourselves and to others about what has happened.

This is always true. And it's true of *all* the stories we tell.

If you tell yourself that you are bad at math, you will have a harder time calculating the tip at a restaurant. If you tell yourself that you are clumsy, you are more likely to trip over your shoelaces. It works the other way too. Tell yourself that you are an expert, and you will seem more confident to others, regardless of your actual level of expertise. Accuracy, as it turns out, is sometimes less important than meaning.

The meaning of the story lies in the *why* of it. And we can tell many different versions that attempt to capture the why of something. Even the simplest stories we tell reveal important beliefs we hold *both* about ourselves and the world.

Let's go back to your favorite mug. When you tell the story of it plummeting to the floor, which of the following versions do you use?

Version A: Because I was in a rush and wasn't being careful.

Version B: Because the universe is out to get me.

Version C: Because I'm clumsy and am always doing things like this, and this is why I can't have nice things.

Version D: Because I was mean to my brother last night, and karma likes my brother better.

Each version reveals something important about the story you're telling about yourself and the world. In Version A, you recognize that you behaved without care, and the consequence is that your mug broke.

Your stance about the world is that this kind of thing happens sometimes. In Version B, you believe that you are not to blame for your actions and are perpetually a victim of some higher malevolent force that has you in its crosshairs. Your stance about the world is that we are locked in a battle and you will always lose. In Version C, you're taking responsibility for the mug breaking, but in an overly general way. Instead of noticing you were behaving recklessly *in that moment*, you're holding this story up as proof that you are fundamentally flawed. The only way to correct this flaw is by not allowing yourself to have nice things. That way, when you're clumsy and break things, you will care less. In Version D, you are taking responsibility indirectly—not for the mug breaking, but for a previous transgression. The role of the universe is to keep tabs and mete out punishment or reward accordingly.

If the stories we tell ourselves about minor events reflect how we see the world and ourselves, imagine the stories of more significant events: Your wife left you. Your young, healthy dog died. You lost your job for no reason.

When an event in our lives seems to have *no* rhyme or reason, it's hard to tell a story about it. And this causes a problem. An unwritten story cannot be integrated, which reflects on the entire story arc of your identity and your life. Suddenly, it's not just that you don't know what this *thing* means. You don't know what *you* mean. You can't integrate *this* story into *your* story, and so you stop being able to understand yourself altogether. Suddenly, the story of your life has been rewritten in a language you do not speak, and you're left with a beat-up, pocket-sized translation dictionary that can teach you how to ask where the bathroom is but has no entries for "existential dread."

This is where Malcolm was. He couldn't make sense of the fact that he got out alive, and so he couldn't make sense of his life. And he couldn't make sense of the universe. It's not the fact that he went to war that was traumatic, it's the fact that he *came back*. Ironically, his survival is what threw off his story and drove him to risk his marriage, his consciousness, and his life. He made it out of combat alive, but if he was going to make it out of coming home alive, he was going to need a different story to tell.

Here's the hopeful part: since we are the authors and narrators of our experience, we can change our stories. When we change our stories, we change the world we live in and how we live in it.

How do we do that? It's easier than you think. You just have to let go of the belief that there is only one version of your story.

TRAUMA TOOL: FOUR VERSIONS OF YOUR STORY

For this exercise, you'll need to choose an event in your life that you are struggling with, or an event you think might be getting in the way of your progress. I'll outline the steps and then use Malcolm's story as an example to illustrate how to do them.

Step 1: Facts. Write down the *facts* of the story without any interpretive data and as simply as possible. Think of yourself as an objective reporter or a video camera, simply recounting what you saw.

Step 2: Four Interpretations. Write four different interpretations of this event and why it happened. At least one (and likely more than one) should be an interpretation you either believe is true or worry might be true. These interpretations should be brief— about a paragraph or two long. It is not at all important whether you *believe* all these interpretations. The power of the exercise is in simply writing them down.

Step 3: Meaning of Each Interpretation. When you've listed your interpretations, write one to two sentences about what each interpretation means for you and the world.

Step 4: Somatic Perspectives. When you're done, read each interpretation out loud. Take some notes about how you feel in your body when you read these stories back to yourself. Do the versions bring up feelings of anxiety? Of peace?

Here's what Malcolm might write if he did this exercise.

Step 1: Facts. I enlisted in the military and was deployed to both Iraq and Afghanistan multiple times over three years. While there were many close calls, and I lost many fellow service members, I survived and have been struggling since I came home. I especially struggle with the randomness of it all—that I survived and get to live longer while many did not and cannot.

Step 2: Four Interpretations.

Interpretation A: There is no rhyme or reason to the universe and it is simply random good luck that I survived. I should feel lucky and not guilty.

Interpretation B: There has been a great cosmic mistake and it should have been me who was killed instead of my friends. My lot in life is to carry this guilt until I die.

Interpretation C: I was spared because there is something that I need to accomplish, but because I'm having trouble figuring out what that is, I'm failing the universe.

Interpretation D: There is likely a rhyme and reason to the universe, but since we are flawed and finite human beings, we do not get access to it. The universe and these circumstances don't make sense to me, but that doesn't mean they don't make sense at all. Since we don't get access to it, the best we can do is do the best we can.

Step 3: Meaning of Each Interpretation.

Interpretation A: In this version, I am not responsible for my successes or my failures, and the world is random and chaotic.

Interpretation B: In this version, my existence is a mistake. The universe is all-powerful but also makes mistakes, and we are left to suffer from the consequences.

Interpretation C: In this version, the universe has given me an important role and then kept that role a secret, making me responsible for figuring out why I am here and what I am supposed to do with my life but not empowering me to do that.

Interpretation D: In this version, there is the idea that there's an organizing force in the universe and the understanding that we can't always make sense of that organizing force. Since all we can do is the best we can do, I just have to try to live my life in the best way possible.

Step 4: Somatic Perspectives.

Interpretation A: This version brings up a lot of feelings of anxiety and restlessness. It feels like there is no hope or way forward.

Interpretation B: This version brings up some anger and frustration. It feels like life is some sort of cosmic joke, which is demoralizing.

Interpretation C: This version brings up some feelings of exhaustion and, again, frustration. The idea of unfairness keeps coming up. There's also some franticness because there must be a way to look for signs that can show me which way is the right direction.

Interpretation D: This version makes me feel like I can take a deep breath. My shoulders relax and my jaw unclenches. It makes sense that there might be an order we don't get to fully know. That belief makes me feel like the path is stretched out in front of me and I must keep going.

This exercise has two goals. The first is to simply occupy different external perspectives repeatedly. Each time we do this, we send a message to ourselves that the event we're trying to sort out is in the past. Hearing this message can make the event feel like less of a present danger even when we're not yet settled on a particular interpretation over another.

The second goal is to empower ourselves to consider alternative perspectives of our story. This helps us to see that though there are a great many things in the world that are outside of our control, we do have some control when it comes to assigning meaning to those things.

Though this exercise can be expansive and can help us see that we might be holding on to a harmful and limiting story, it's important to keep in mind that it might not banish those harmful and limiting versions right away. That's okay. It's normal for the old version to come floating into your consciousness in a moment of stress or uncertainty. Just because a thought is rattling around up there does not mean you need to let it stick. As the great bumper sticker proclaims, "Don't believe everything you think."

CHAPTER 3

Gabe's Broken Heart
The Truth about Triggers

The painter "takes his body with him." . . . Indeed, we cannot
imagine how a mind could paint. It is by lending his body to
the world that the artist changes the world into paintings.

Maurice Merleau-Ponty

Fifteen minutes into my first session with Gabe, he starts to hyperventilate. He's taking short, shallow breaths, and his shoulders rise dramatically with each one. He can only get through two or three words before he has to take another breath. I interrupt him.

"Hey, this is going to sound a little odd, but let's pause here. Could you lie down on the floor for a second? I want to try a quick breathing exercise with you."

Without even the slightest hesitation, Gabe gets out of his chair, shifts his camera, and lies down on the floor. The lack of hesitation does not surprise me. We met only fifteen minutes ago, but I know the look in his eyes intimately. Distrust of others is a luxury you can't often afford when you have lost the ability to trust your own body. If I told him being upside down would help him feel less anxious, he would be trying to kick into a handstand before the sentence was fully out of my mouth. I recognize this look in his eyes because I've been on the other side of it. It is a kind of terrible that escapes language.

I ask Gabe to take a big deep breath and notice where it goes. When you're lying on the floor, your breath more naturally goes into your belly, which activates your parasympathetic nervous system, the branch of the nervous system responsible for calming the body. Just two minutes of breathing into your belly will lower your heart rate and stabilize your blood pressure. I breathe with him for a couple of minutes, and we count. Inhale to the count of four, hold for two, exhale to the count of five.

When he gets back in his chair, Gabe's face is relaxed and his eyes are wide.

"Wow! That makes a big difference," he says, putting his hand to his chest as if he's wondering where all this space came from.

"I know it," I say. "I was surprised when I first tried that too. Do you often notice yourself breathing shallow and quick like that?"

"No, not all the time. Maybe fifteen times a day or so? I guess about half of the day. Mmm, maybe all the time."

Now, without hyperventilating, Gabe starts to tell me more about why he came to see me. His father died at the age of forty-three, when Gabe was just ten. His dad had a heart condition that no one knew about. He had a heart attack in the living room while Gabe stood in the doorway, stunned.

As if that weren't enough, Gabe inherited the same heart condition. Being born with a broken heart is hard to understand at the age of ten, and so Gabe adapted by living most of his life without thinking about it. This coping technique worked great until Gabe had his own heart attack at twenty-seven. Then, his heart became a whole lot harder to ignore.

Technological advances mean that Gabe is far, far less likely to die prematurely, as his father did. He's had a tiny defibrillator implanted in his chest. It is designed to shock his heart when it stops, saving his life. But there's a catch: the device can malfunction and shock his heart when it hasn't stopped. It is not a small shock, either. People describe it as feeling like being kicked by a horse directly in the chest. The shock can make you pass out, and sometimes the machine shocks several times in a row in what is called an electrical storm. This storm isn't just unpleasant—it can kill you. So when it happens, it comes with the terrible understanding that this awful feeling might be the last feeling you ever have.

Gabe has coped with everything else—the death of his father, his own heart attack, and the radical lifestyle changes he had to make afterward, plus the surgery needed to implant the little machine in his chest. But a handful of electrical storms have sent him over the edge. After experiencing an episode that sent him careening across the floor of his apartment and knocked him unconscious, he found himself completely unable to relax—ever.

There is a wild and layered irony to all of this. Just like the defibrillator that is designed to keep him alive but can still malfunction, Gabe's amygdala, part of his body's trauma response team, is going off when he's not actually in danger and is threatening his psychological stability. In both cases, the very thing that is there to keep Gabe alive is making his life unlivable.

Hypervigilance, a state of increased alertness, is one of the most common symptoms of PTSD. We see hypervigilance depicted by the media through a war veteran who cannot stop scanning the room for danger even though they are in their own home, or a sexual assault survivor who startles and nearly faints when their roommate pops into the kitchen to ask a question. Though there is no present danger, the person with hypervigilance cannot bear to relax. The traumatic experience has written itself into the body. Trauma has revealed the world to be fundamentally dangerous in a way that biology will not forget.

Gabe came to me because although there's a lot you can learn on the internet about trauma, loss, and the strange organ at our center that keeps rhythm, there is not a lot about what to do when you find yourself triggered by your own heartbeat. We were both in awe of this diabolical duality.

TRIGGERS AND TRAUMATIC MEMORIES

One of the biggest failures of the language of trauma is that we refer to traumatic memories as memories. As if they look or feel like all the rest of our memories. As if we had control over them. Traumatic memories are not memories; they are instances of unwilling and unbidden *reliving*. When we remember, we have cognitive control. We have access to the parts of our brain that can think rationally. And while we may feel some of the emotions related to the memory, we typically can put the memory and emotions away when we need to.

Reliving, on the other hand, is not something we do, it is something that happens to us. It puts us back into the time of the trauma. Trauma victims learn the horrible trick of occupying two temporalities simultaneously—as past and present toggle like near and far sight. This kind of toggling may look fun in sci-fi movies, but it can make our lives a literal living hell.

The only other word we have for this kind of whiplash memory and the cascade of biological responses that come with it is *trigger*. Unfortunately, the word *trigger* has been nearly stretched to utter meaninglessness. It was once a term designed to refer to these strange nonmemory memories but has become a catchall for any occasion in which we have an emotion that is remotely unpleasant or unwanted. We talk about being triggered by not getting what we want in relationships or by people who hold political beliefs that oppose our own. These experiences are valid and important and worthy of discussion. But we need a more appropriate nomenclature to refer to them, because when we homogenize them in this way, using the same inappropriate word to capture them, we do them *all* an injustice.

Our misconception of what it means to be triggered is especially dangerous because it has led us to misunderstand what we should do when it happens. We have learned, or mislearned, to block and avoid, to annihilate instead of adapt or heal. Once someone utters the phrase, "I'm triggered," hands go up in surrender and conversation shuts down.

Sometimes people really are triggered. Often, they are not. We need to get better at understanding the difference. And we need to recognize that in *either* case, surrender and shutdown are signs of collapse, not signs of health and integration.

If we mistake reliving for remembering, and remembering for reliving, and any feeling as triggering, and triggering as a cue to collapse, we misunderstand the very core of traumatic experience and we fail to heal.

AVOIDING THE TRIGGER TRAP

In today's discussion of trauma and triggers, three ideas have been coming up with more and more frequency, and all three are dangerous to our understanding and treatment of trauma.

The first is the idea that we are always conscious of our triggers and can effectively communicate about them—that we can identify when we're triggered and say, "I'm triggered." The second is the idea that triggers are to be avoided at all costs by both those who suffer from them and those who do not. Closely related to this point is the third idea, which is that you have properly annihilated a trigger (and are therefore healed) when you feel absolutely *nothing* when you are reminded of what traumatized you. All three of these ideas are incorrect and reflect a woefully inaccurate understanding of how triggers and memory work. Let me explain why each of these ideas is wrong and what the truth is.

First, we do not always have the ability to consciously identify our triggers or what they are tied to. Our triggers are about survival, and so they sometimes slip past our awareness. Often, we feel bad for reasons that we cannot seem to explain. I am a person who knows this truth. I have dedicated my life to studying trauma, and it took me a *full five years* to realize that the reason I couldn't bear to eat, smell, or be near spaghetti with tomato sauce is that it was the last meal my father ate before he went into the hospital and died ten days later. I had no conscious awareness that my brain had connected tomato sauce with danger and *that connection* was what was making me so nauseous. I just knew I could no longer eat something I used to love.

Triggers are portals to the past. When the portals are open, the past comes flooding forward, unbidden. The word *portal* comes from the Latin word *porta*, meaning "entrance, passage, or door." It refers not to any old door, but an imposing one, like a gate to a city. Portals allow access to cities; citizens sweep through them in times of celebration and back out during times of disaster. There is even a portal vein, which carries blood in and out the liver, keeping the body alive. Unfiltered blood comes spilling into the liver, filtered blood goes spilling back out.

Portals aren't always passageways to something pleasant, but they are biologically necessary.

Anything—including imperceptible internal states like fluctuations in your heart rate—can be a trigger, a portal opening to a set of imprinted, vivid fragments from the past. And through this, the past comes rushing through like blood rushing into the liver. Being triggered is different than simply feeling an emotion. It involves being thrown back into the past in a way that is entirely outside of your control. Having an unpleasant sensation or emotion is simply not the same as being shot through a portal to the terror and annihilation of the past while sitting comfortably on your couch. Having a particular feeling might be inconvenient or unpleasant, but not all feelings cause your body to be flooded with stress hormones. Being inconvenienced or upset is simply not the same thing as being triggered.

The second truth is that triggers do not exist to remind us of what we should avoid. They exist so that we *do not* forget, so that we integrate what has so far gone unintegrated. They are signs that there are things that we have not yet processed, signs there is work to be done. They are not pleasant, but we need them.

The third truth is that *not feeling anything is not a realistic goal*. Integration is the goal. You know that you've integrated something when you can narrate the event, feel *some* of the emotions tied to it, assign that event meaning, and put the memory down when you want to. If we think that any undesirable feeling is a trigger, we then make the mistake of thinking healing has occurred when we stop feeling altogether. We can learn how to de-escalate and intervene in our nervous systems' responses when we are exposed to triggers, but we can't do this by avoiding them altogether.

REMEMBERING AND RELIVING

Let's start from the beginning: Our brains process different events in different ways. In our day-to-day lives, events occur, and for the most part they make sense. We go to work, have conversations, tell jokes, get frustrated, and have arguments. All of this gets encoded and filed away appropriately, primarily in a part of the brain called the hippocampus. The memory files stored in the hippocampus contain three things: a coherent narrative of the event, emotional content from that event, and a set of tags or labels that indicate what the event means to us. For most life events, we have relatively organized files that we can pull when we need to. We can relate the contents to other people, feel some of the emotional content—the maniacal laughter, the bittersweet sadness— and then put the file back and go on with our day.

If someone tells a joke at work, for example, you remember the joke and tag the file with the meaning "funny work story." You may come home at the end of the day and retell it. You will likely smile or laugh as you do, feeling some of the emotional content that accompanied the original event. Or you might forget about it that night and tell the story three days later. Or the memory might pop up again three years later, when other people are relaying similar stories. In all these cases, your conscious mind is in control.

When you experience something overwhelming, however, the recording mechanisms in your brain go a little haywire, and as a result, the file is created, but is disorganized in one of many possible ways.

It is critical to note that this atypical organization is *by design*. The brain has evolved to recognize and respond to threatening situations differently than nonthreatening ones. This filing method is both more efficient and more likely to keep us alive. Think of it this way: In *nonthreatening* situations, your brain does not need to go through threat protocols. In *threatening* situations, your brain does not need to create complicated files for your memories; it needs to lock and load.

The brain structures behind this process are the amygdala and the brain stem. We can think of the amygdala as an alarm system. It is constantly scanning for threats, and when one appears, it sets off an alarm. The brain stem responds to the alarm by sending out stress hormones that reprioritize brain and body function to prepare for the threat, respond effectively to the danger, and stay alive.

If you have ever been awoken to a crash in the middle of the night, you have experienced this response system. You likely shot up in bed fully alert despite the fact that a second ago you were in a deep sleep. Your heart rate immediately went up, your blood pressure rose, and stress hormones went coursing through your body like mentholated bees.

Since we have limited energy stores and capacity, the reprioritization of function is critical. Think of your nervous system as a command center. When the stress response system is activated, certain knobs are turned way up and others are turned way down. Functions that are less important in a moment of threat are turned down so that more energy can be sent to support functions that are more important. Less important functions in a moment of threat are digestion, reproduction, rational processing, and memory encoding. More important functions are movement, perception, and strength. You might feel silly if you jump out of bed wielding a heavy flashlight like a weapon before you realize that the sound that woke you up was the dog's sleep apnea. But the systems that make this possible are the same ones that make you feel like a hero when you suddenly have the superhuman strength needed to lift a car off your child. This sophisticated and adaptive system is worthy of awe and appreciation.

There's a somewhat inconvenient upshot of the efficient operation of the threat system: one of the things that gets slowed down is the recording mechanism in your brain. When the amygdala gets flooded, the hippocampus, the part of the brain that forms memories and stores them long term, effectively goes offline. You don't need to be recording and filing the event during the moment of overwhelm, but these tasks do need to happen so that the trauma memory can be filed away just like all your other memories. If it isn't recorded and filed, the trauma memory will stay in the present and manifest itself in symptoms.

When your recording mechanism isn't fully online, instead of a coherent memory file, you get *fragments*—sounds, colors, smells, phrases, tastes—that are filed away in disorganized ways. Just because they are disorganized does not mean that they don't get stored. In fact, they get imprinted deeply. Your brain will hold on to those things at all costs, because again, they represent threat or danger, and we learn our most vivid lessons from fear. Storing fragments of an event is a necessary and positive survival tactic.

The problem is, these fragmented pieces act as triggers—portals that open to the initial trauma and send your stress response system into overdrive, reacting to a threat that is not actually there. By the time you realize you're not actually in danger, your body is already off and running through its survival process.

Here's a quick example. Let's say you get mugged by someone wearing a shirt that is a deep maroon color. During the mugging, your stress response system is activated appropriately. While your hippocampus is still recording the event, its work is far less important than those processes that are tied to survival. It uses the little energy available to it to record whatever details of the event it can—bits of color, the frantic feeling in your chest as you ran away, the smell of the night air, the black-rimmed glasses worn by the mugger. It saves those pieces, but they're just sort of thrown into a cabinet. They're not organized and neatly filed away like the rest of your memories.

Since these memory fragments are so disorganized, you relive them every time a reminder pushes one of them to the surface rather than being able to pull them into consciousness and talk about them at your own will. Sometimes the reliving is prompted by an internal state (like an elevated heart rate when going for a jog), and sometimes it is prompted by something in the external world (the smell of someone's cologne or the way the light falls at dusk). If you're at work and someone walks by wearing a shirt that's the exact same deep maroon color the mugger wore, you may feel all the adrenaline rushing back. The stress response system is reactivated because it has recorded that color as part of the very real threat that you lived through. When you encounter it again, it signals your brain and body to set off the same processes that kept you alive the first time. The difference is you're not in danger; you're just sitting at your desk.

Because the alarm signal was so subtle and fast, and because the memory file it is connected to is fragmented, you may not consciously connect that signal with your trauma. Instead of thinking, "Oh, Fred is wearing the same color shirt as the person who mugged me. That reminds me of how scary that mugging was," you'll just panic without knowing why.

This panic is your stress response system kicking into gear even though it doesn't need to. We'll look more closely into why, from a neurobiological perspective, this "hair trigger" happens. For now, know that on a biological level, your brain and body perceive threat and react as if the threat were real because they do not know the difference yet.

It is important to understand that when we talk about "reliving" the past, it is not a poetic turn of phrase meant to emphasize the pain of remembering a traumatic experience and your system's response to it. Your brain and body are actually reliving the past—like, *actually-actually*. When you are exposed to a trigger, your brain and body cannot tell the difference between the present and the past. They think the trauma is happening all over again, and because their response worked successfully the first time (in keeping you alive), they are responding the same way again. While you may have a rational awareness that you are safe at your desk at work, your body is in another realm entirely, fighting for its life.

If triggers are a central experience of trauma, what can we do about them? As it turns out, many things can be done to make the journey through the portal gentler, or even close the portal altogether. Most fall under one of two categories: retelling and reeducating.

RETELLING

Freud and Breuer's first patient, Anna O., had the particularly fascinating symptom of being "transferred into the past." Anna had spent ten months in 1880 taking care of her ailing father as he died. Whenever she smelled oranges, which she had eaten almost exclusively while taking care of him, Anna would retreat into 1880 with such intensity that she forgot nearly every detail of the following years, including the fact that she had moved. She would fully hallucinate her old room so vividly that she would try to open the door, only to find herself standing in front of the stove.

After spending several months with her, Breuer stumbled on a therapeutic procedure that he claimed rid her of these symptoms. He was trying to deal with one of the more urgent symptoms, hydrophobia, a fear and repulsion of water that is so intense, the patient stops drinking water altogether. Anna would feel thirsty, reach for a glass of water, and then push it away, unable to drink. She had no conscious understanding of why she was suddenly hydrophobic.

One evening, while under hypnosis, Anna started to tell a story about a visiting friend who let her dog drink out of her own water glass. Anna had felt it necessary to be polite in the moment, but under hypnosis she revealed feeling intense repulsion and disgust. As soon as she expressed those emotions, she asked for a glass of water, drank it, and then awoke from the hypnosis session, never to experience hydrophobia again.

Though seeing a dog drink from her friend's water glass wasn't necessarily traumatic, Anna had felt intense emotion that could not be expressed at the time, which led to an interruption in her normal functioning. Talking through the unprocessed emotions had stopped them from bursting into the present unbidden.

In subsequent conversations with Anna while she was under hypnosis, Breuer took each of her symptoms and connected it with the original disturbance. He reported that as they went through this process, each symptom disappeared. As he says, "In this way her paralytic contractors and anesthesias, disorders of vision and hearing of every sort, neuralgias, coughing, tremors, etc., and finally her disturbances of speech were 'talked away.'"[1]

Aha! So if the patient could be convinced to talk about the traumatic event while feeling the overwhelming emotions that were repressed, the traumatic symptoms no longer had any need to manifest themselves somatically. Sort out the underlying memory, and the trigger loses its power.

If triggers are portals to traumatic memories, narrating the traumatic event with a therapist is helpful because it provides a way to walk through the portal slowly and sort out what is there. When you tell a story, you render an event into story form. You add cohesion and structure to it, making sure it has a beginning, middle, and end. You make it coherent. Telling the story allows for missing pieces to be filled in (sometimes by the imagination) and allows you to take an external perspective of the event.

When we render a traumatic event into story form, it starts to look like the rest of our memories. Memories that are organized in this way are recognizable as events from the past. When we retell the events, the memory fragments our brain had hastily stuffed into its filing system in a haphazard, disorganized way become organized into a coherent memory. We pick up the scattered pieces like papers that had been dropped on the floor, put them in the correct order and right side up, and straighten the edges of the pile. Our brain can now file the whole memory neatly alongside other coherent memories from innocuous everyday events. We can engage with these memories and their content just as we can engage with the narrative of a piece of fiction. We recognize it as an event from the past, and so we stop needing to relive it. Rather than continuing to be shot into the past, we begin to be able to navigate the portal with some control.

There are many, many ways to begin this retelling process, but the best place to start is with someone you can trust to help bring you back to your baseline if you end up getting truly triggered. The tricky thing in working with trauma narratives is that when we open the portal, the overwhelm comes rushing through and can shut us down all over again. Not only is it impossible to get any helpful work done in that state, but it can also make it more likely that we end up chronically activated. So it's critical that we do this work in the presence of someone who can recognize what it looks like when we get triggered and who knows what to do to help us calm down. That could be a spiritual advisor, a trusted therapist, or a coach who is well versed in trauma. Look for therapists that list "trauma" as an area of focus and "narrative therapy" as one of their treatment approaches.

REEDUCATING

Retelling stories didn't seem to be the issue with Gabe, though. He could tell his stories coherently—the story of his father's death, of his own diagnosis, of his treatment, and of his experience with electrical storms. It's just that whenever he did so, he found himself triggered.

In his case, the narrative wasn't the issue. It's what the narrative *meant* that was problematic. It wasn't the narrative part of the memory file; it was the meaning tags on the file.

You'll remember from earlier in the chapter that each memory file contains three things: a narrative of the event, emotional content from the event, and a set of tags or labels that assign meaning to the event. Since memory files can become fragmented in so many ways, it is not always the narrative that is disrupted. Sometimes the narrative is perfectly coherent, but the emotional content is fragmented. Other times the narrative and the emotional content are in place, but the tags and labels don't fit the event properly.

These fragmentations can look like a thousand things. When the emotional content is in order, you might feel some of the emotions tied to a memory when you think about it. Tears might come to your eyes when you talk about the day your father died, for example, but you are still mostly in control and can move on and continue functioning after a few minutes. When the emotional content is not in order, telling or thinking about the story (even though the narrative is intact) either causes extreme activation or complete shutdown. You might try to talk about the day your father died and end up in a panic attack, hyperventilating and sobbing. Or you might be able to talk about it in extreme and shocking detail while registering no emotion at all, feeling only cold and dark indifference. Both extremes are a result of emotional content that has not been integrated.

When the tags and labels are in order, you can tell a story and convey its meaning—both what it means to you as an individual and what it means about the external world. Fragmentation can be more difficult to recognize in this case, but sweeping distress is a good indication that the meaning of an event has not been integrated into your larger life story and your story about the world. If a memory of a mistake brings a cascade of shame and a belief that you are bad or unworthy or broken, that memory needs some reintegrating. The same is true if the memory of the day your father died relates to a suffocating belief that the world is inherently full of suffering and without hope.

It's critical to note here that though this memory stuff might sound damning, *any* of these fragmentations in memory files can be worked with and sorted out. We will talk more about this in chapter 4, but the point is, we have a lot more power than we may think when it comes to reorganizing memory files.

Since Gabe had spent so many years refusing to think about what his father's death and his own resulting heart condition meant for him and his life, he hadn't assigned meaning tags to these events. That is why signing on to our session and beginning to tell his story triggered a panic that was palpable through a computer screen. He could tell the story, but his brain wasn't sure how to put it back in the filing system. So, to protect him, his brain assumed he was in danger and responded accordingly.

What do you do if you've done the work of retelling (narrating) and are still triggered? Reeducation, that's what.

In the 1940s, trauma researcher Abram Kardiner realized that there was something critical going on that had not yet been accounted for. It was not just that a traumatic event left behind confusing and unexpressed emotions; the event changed the way the patient experienced the world altogether. Kardiner recognized that trauma and the symptoms that follow make us feel radically unsafe in the world and in our bodies *in general*—not simply in moments when we are triggered, but *all the time.*

He also recognized that it was not always just a matter of helping patients process what had happened, but of reeducating them about reality. Kardiner wrote, "Every effort should be bent to re-educating the patient to the *actual realities* in which he lives rather than to the dangerous and inhospitable world in which he fancies himself."[2] Although the trauma response activated because of a specific event, traumatic injury is global. It is a wound in which one loses their sense of safety in the world altogether.

One of Kardiner's case studies was a veteran whose primary symptom was fainting. Every time the man was in an elevator or ran up the stairs of his apartment building too quickly, he would faint. He also had terrible nightmares of falling from high places and would wake up each night in a cold sweat. Assuming the fainting indicated an issue in his blood pressure, he had gone to the doctor. They couldn't find anything physically wrong, but the symptom would not go away and was disrupting his life significantly.

In working with the veteran, Kardiner discovered the man had survived a helicopter crash during his deployment. While his helicopter was hurtling through the air, he had fainted, a completely natural defense mechanism that likely saved his life. Sometimes called the "ragdoll effect," this mechanism of the nervous system makes people go limp just before impact in an accident. When the body is limp on impact, it's far more likely that the person will survive. This veteran could talk about the crash coherently and completely dismissed the idea that he had been psychologically traumatized by it. Many people had been through worse, and he felt lucky to have survived.

Despite the fact that the patient had nightmares of falling *every* night, despite the fact that the pit in his stomach before he fainted was the *same exact* feeling he'd had when his helicopter was plummeting through the air, and despite the fact that his symptom was so clearly tied to this event, he *still* did not cognitively connect these symptoms to the crash because he didn't think his experience had been traumatic. His symptom was physical, not psychological, so they couldn't be connected. Nor did he *want* them to be connected. Remember, at the time, to be suffering from combat trauma was to be constitutionally and fundamentally weak.

Just like Gabe, this veteran was being triggered by an imperceptible *internal state*. When he experienced fluctuations in his blood pressure, he was shot through the trauma portal all over again. But since he couldn't identify the physical state with the traumatic event, he couldn't understand why he was still being tortured.

We do not choose our triggers, nor do we always have conscious access to them.

Kardiner helped this patient by gradually convincing him of two things: First, that the experience of fainting when going up the stairs or riding in an elevator was connected to the helicopter crash. He had to show the patient that the portal was there in the first place. Second, that though fainting had likely saved him in the first place, there was no need to hold on to that response for the rest of his life. The patient had to be reeducated to reality and shown that "these defensive devices *were quite irrelevant to the actual world in which he was living.*"[3] The defensive devices were not *wrong*, they were just no longer relevant. The patient's natural defense mechanism had come to accompany experiences in the world in which *there was no actual danger*. To heal, the patient needed to see that though the traumatic event was indeed terrifying, he need not be terrified all the time.

The body, in an earnest and endearing effort to ensure survival, makes the mistake of assuming that the best way to survive is to remain fixed on the potential danger that just might be lurking around the corner. The result is that you are hypervigilant and uncomfortable all the time. Traumatic events do not just create a disorganized memory file; they stamp the world with indelible meaning. Healing trauma, then, is not just about retelling and reorganizing memories; it is also about coming to understand how the traumatic event has changed your reality.

I need you to understand that *the trauma response is never wrong*. The automatic defenses that kick in exactly when we need them come from a sophisticated system designed to save our lives. What causes distress is the way we understand and respond to these responses—when we judge them or try to banish them, when we use them to reify a story that we are weak or broken or that the world is fundamentally hopeless.

When Anna smelled oranges, she was sent through a portal to the year she watched her father die in front of her eyes. She was reminded that those she loves can and will die. When Kardiner's veteran experienced any fluctuation in his blood pressure, he was sent through a portal back to the moment that his helicopter went into freefall. His body perceived the threat and responded by repeating what it had done to keep him alive during the crash. When Gabe's heart flutters, he is sent through a set of portals back to the moment his father died, the moment he received his own diagnosis, the moment of his heart attack, and the moment his body was seized by electrical storms. For Gabe, each of these portals bears the same meaning: that life is precarious—and his life even more so than most.

Here's the thing, though: Gabe is right and wrong. Life is precarious and maybe his life is even more so than most. But the answer to precarity is *not* to live in constant fear. Reeducating his body to understand that he is not in danger all the time is going to be critical to his healing process. This reeducation happens when you work on two planes: with the memory file and with the body. You can work on these planes simultaneously, or you can do one and then the other. If you want to work simultaneously, look for a therapist who specializes in trauma and lists "narrative therapy" *and* "somatic therapy." Alternatively, you can start working with a therapist on the retelling while you use some of the workbooks in the Recommended Resources section to begin reeducating the body.

TAKEAWAYS AND TOOLS

The trauma response is *never* wrong, but it *is* really frustrating sometimes. This is because it carries inside of it a tension that cannot be resolved—a diabolical duality. David Morris, a veteran and war correspondent, captures this perfectly when he writes, "Trauma is the glimpse of truth that tells us a lie: the lie that love is impossible, that peace is an illusion."[4]

Trauma is the glimpse of truth that tells us a lie.

The truth is, we are all terminally vulnerable. Our existence and all the things we hold dear within it are haunted by this vulnerability. Everything is precarious. We spend most of our lives holding this truth at bay. We keep busy and act as if it were not true. Traumatic events rupture our lives and reveal this terrible truth with a vividness that cannot be ignored. And yet this moment of rupture is not the whole story. Trauma does not restrict itself to a moment. It is more powerful than that. It spills through portals into the present, reinforcing the lie that trauma tells us: That terror is the foundation of everything. That terror is the only thing that exists. That once we have seen this terror, we must never lose our focus on it. That this kind of hypervigilance is the only way to live.

Gabe's struggle is not just that he has panic attacks when he tells his story, or that he is triggered by fluctuations in his heart rate. It is that his trauma has taught him that he is unsafe, that death awaits around every corner, and that the answer is to be forever vigilant so you can at least be prepared. Gabe doesn't simply need to tell his story and relive it. He's done that. He needs to learn how to hold a staggering contradiction: that he is vulnerable (more so than most) and he is also safe.

Humans are traditionally piss-poor at holding two contradictory thoughts at the same time, but Gabe and I are working on it. And we're doing lots of breathing exercises as we go.

TRAUMA AND BOTTOM-UP REGULATION

We talk about psychological struggle as if it were possible to compartmentalize, as if the body were not involved, as if all the sorting and healing that needs to be done occurs in the prefrontal cortex and the prefrontal cortex alone. We are wrong. The body is *very* much along for the ride, present and reacting to every thought, marking every experience in a complex topography.

The nervous system is the cartographer, carefully mapping experiences on flesh and taking note of the geography of your body and what flourishes where. Constriction and heaviness in your chest signify being trapped and silenced. A roiling, upset gut signifies being nervous and unheard. Gripping tension in your neck signifies being overwhelmed and without an end in sight.

Although the idea that the body is along for the ride may sound ominous, it is not. The body is not permanently stuck on this rollercoaster ride, and knowing more about the nervous system makes it possible to intervene in automatic responses when they are not useful.

Bottom-up regulation is when you use the body to regulate the responses in the brain, which can then intervene in the stress response. The quickest way to do this is to flip the switch from the sympathetic nervous system to the parasympathetic nervous system.

As you'll recall from the neurobiology primer in chapter 1, there are two branches of the autonomic nervous system (ANS): the sympathetic nervous system (SNS), which is responsible for activation, and the parasympathetic nervous system (PNS), which is responsible for rest and relaxation. When we are activated—by either a current threat or a memory of a threat—the brain stem sends up a flare, and the sympathetic nervous system kicks into high gear, increasing our alertness, energy, heart rate, and breathing rate. You need these physical reactions to handle the threat in front of you and survive. Once the threat is over, the parasympathetic nervous system kicks into gear, slowing that activation back down so that you can rest again. It acts a bit like a parachute (also a good way to remember what each branch does—*para*sympathetic, *para*chute). When you pull the ripcord, it takes over and glides you gently to the ground. Your hands might be shaking from the surge of adrenaline, but you've landed on your feet. You're okay.

The most reliable way to pull the parasympathetic ripcord is by activating the vagus nerve. The vagus nerve is the largest nerve in your body, owing its name to the Latin word *vagus*, meaning "to wander." The nerve wanders from your brain stem through your abdomen and touches nearly all of your major organs on the way down. It is innervated—meaning it has lots and lots of nerve endings—in two places: in the back of the throat, where it leaves the brain stem and begins its path downward, and in front of your belly. This gives us two places where we can activate the vagus nerve and trigger a parasympathetic (calming) response in the body. When we do this in the presence of something that the brain has mistakenly interpreted as a threat, we can interrupt the stress response and return to a state of calm.

TRAUMA TOOL: DIAPHRAGMATIC BREATHING FOR VAGAL RESPONSE

Since one of the places that the vagus nerve has most of its nerve endings is in the stomach, there is a very simple tool you can use to activate the parasympathetic response at any time: diaphragmatic breathing.

When we are stressed, we often breathe like Gabe when he signed on for our first session—shallow, quick breaths into the upper chest that expand the rib cage and lift the shoulders. This kind of breath pattern, sometimes called "high costal breathing" (*costal* for ribs), will *not* activate the vagus nerve. Instead, we need to do two things: breathe into the diaphragm and breathe slowly and steadily.

The diaphragm is a large muscle that sits right below your lungs. When you breathe and focus on the muscles in the middle of your abdomen, rather than your chest and upper lungs, you should feel your abdomen muscles engage. The diaphragm moves downward, making space for your lungs to fill completely. As you exhale slowly, the diaphragm relaxes and moves upward, helping to move the air out of your lungs. This is the kind of breathing singers use to get full use of their lung capacity and project their voice to the back of a theater. Breathing this way pushes against the vagus nerve, manually triggering its parasympathetic response, which will deactivate the sympathetic response and bring calm into your body.

You will know if you are breathing diaphragmatically if you notice the middle of your stomach rising and falling rather than your chest and shoulders. If you cannot seem to direct your breath away from the top of your lungs, lie on your back on the floor with your knees up and your feet flat on the ground. This position will naturally send your breath into your stomach. This is why I asked Gabe to lie on the floor to breathe; I could see that his default breathing was not diaphragmatic, and I wanted him to be able to feel the effects quickly. Once you know what diaphragmatic breathing feels like, you can try it standing up.

You typically need to take three to six slow, steady diaphragmatic breaths to activate the vagal response. You can try it now using these steps.

Step 1: Take a moment to simply notice what you are feeling in your body. Does your heart rate feel high? Do you feel amped and stressed out? Locate yourself in space, feeling the chair or floor beneath you, supporting you.

Step 2: Take a deep, slow breath in, trying to aim it into the middle of your stomach and expanding your middle as far as you can. Your diaphragm is right below your rib cage, and if you breathe into it, your chest and shoulders should move very little, if at all.

Step 3: Hold this breath in expansion for two or three seconds if you can. Feel the muscles of your abdomen and the strength of the air you've taken in.

Step 4: Exhale slowly and fully, pushing the muscles of your mid-abdomen in and toward each other—as if someone were tightening a corset around your waist.

Step 5: Repeat this same pattern three to six times.

Step 6: Take note of what you are feeling in your body now and how it has shifted from when you began. You will likely feel markedly calmer and might notice less tension in your body.

If you practice this kind of breathing two or three times a day, you will start noticing an increase in calm. You are buffering your system from everyday stressors—whether those stressors are from traumatic memories or not. You can practice this breathing *anytime* you want to get the benefit of the parasympathetic response; you do not have to wait until you are panicked.

Remember: no matter how bad you feel, no matter what you are going through, you are three to six breaths away from feeling just a little calmer, a little more peaceful, and a little more in control. Trauma may have made you feel disconnected from yourself, but your breath and your body are *always* there for you.

TRAUMA TOOL: GROUNDING EXERCISES

There's a second coping tool hidden within the previous one. I explained above that if you can't seem to locate your diaphragm, you should lie on the floor. Not only does lying on the floor make it easier to bring breath into the right spot for vagal response, but as you might remember from the introduction, it qualifies as its own grounding exercise.

In general, grounding is a therapeutic technique used to help you cope with overwhelm. It's called *grounding* because that is its aim: to ground you, to bring you back into the present, anchor you to the moment, and stop the swirling, overwhelming emotions that are staging a hostile takeover. Intense emotions tend to separate us from our bodies, but grounding back into our bodies can help dissipate the intensity of those emotions. Grounding exercises are designed to intervene on the stress response system and, when practiced often, can help you learn to regulate your body's response over time. This can be an enormous help when it comes to managing traumatic memories, panic, and the havoc that these things can wreak on the body.

Grounding exercises can sometimes feel silly but are often wildly effective. They can be practiced anytime and anywhere, usually without anyone else knowing what you're doing. So it's a great idea to add a couple of them to your toolbox for when you're in the middle of a meeting or stuck in traffic. Remember: grounding works for any overwhelming emotion! Use a grounding exercise whenever you're feeling stressed, irritable, or distracted.

Here are four of my favorite grounding exercises.

> **Seated body scan.** Begin by sitting with both feet on the floor. It doesn't matter how you sit in terms of your posture, but make sure that both feet are on the floor. You also may find that sitting on your hands can help you feel more in your body. As you sit, start

noticing the way your body feels. Try to describe in your mind (or out loud, if you can) what the different parts of your body feel, in as much detail as you can. Does the floor feel smooth and cold? Is it warm and soft? Wiggle your toes and think about how they feel in the carpet (or on the tile or wood or whatever). Start to move your attention up your legs and back and describe to yourself how your body feels in the chair. Notice the way your body rests in the chair; notice the way your feet are resting on the floor. Sitting with your feet on the floor is a posture that can allow you to feel both strong and at ease, but you can also do this body scan while lying on the floor, where there's more surface area to feel.

Moving mindfully. Sometimes sitting still is simply not something you can do. If you feel too antsy to sit, that's okay! You can get up and move around and still practice grounding. It doesn't matter if you move slowly or quickly, the key is to pay as much attention as you possibly can to the way it feels to move. If the movement you choose is walking, bring your attention to your feet. Notice how your heels and then the balls of your feet feel as you step forward. Notice the way your weight shifts from one leg to the other as you walk. Notice the noises that your feet make as they move across the floor. When your mind wanders (and it will, and that's just fine), just bring it back to this noticing. If you are having trouble focusing your attention, begin to count your steps as you walk. Count ten steps, and then ten more steps, and then ten more steps until you begin to feel more relaxed and present. If the movement you choose is swaying from left to right in your chair, bring attention to your back or shoulders. Notice how the weight shifts from one side to the other. Where do you feel that in your body? If you are moving in a wheelchair, you might notice how the wheels feel under your fingers, how your arms feel as they move back and forth. Wherever you can bring your attention to, just keep bringing it gently back when it wanders.

Guided imagery. Did you know that our body responds to strong imagery as if it were the real thing? You don't need to *be* in a place of peace in order to *feel* peace. Take a slow, deep breath and, if you can, close your eyes. Picture yourself in a place that makes you feel peace. This might be the house of a loved one or a place that you used to vacation. It can even be a place you've never been. I've never been to a tropical beach, but I love to imagine myself sitting on a white-sand beach with beautiful, crystal-clear water. I imagine hearing the waves gently rolling. I imagine the sunshine on my shoulders, the sounds of birds chirping and children playing. Even just five minutes of visiting my imaginary beach can calm me down and radically shift my mood.

Feel cold, cold water. There's some really interesting (if somewhat conflicting) early data on the impact of cold-water immersion on mental health. Although researchers are still sorting it out, I find applying cold water or ice to my skin to be really, really effective when I'm struggling with anxiety or having a panic attack. In fact, this grounding practice is almost always my first go-to when panic strikes. The general idea is this: get cold water on your skin. Make it as cold as you can stand it—even frozen. Splash cold water on your face or even just your hands. Put ice cubes in your hands or in your mouth. Put an ice pack on your chest, your face, or the back of your neck. Wherever you've got it, however you've got it, focus on the cold. That's your only job—just feel the cold. It'll bring you back down into the moment.

Remember: These grounding exercises work for any overwhelming emotion! Use them when you're feeling stressed or irritable, or when you can't concentrate. If none of these work for you, don't worry—there are thousands out there! If you want more options for grounding, check out the Recommended Resources section for this chapter. I've listed some books that offer additional, science-based grounding practices. You can try others to find which ones work best for you.

CHAPTER 4

Grace's Referred Pain
There Is No Such Thing as Big-T and Little-T Trauma

Pain—has an Element of Blank.

Emily Dickinson

There are a thousand mind-boggling things about pain, and referred pain is one of them. Referred pain is the phenomenon whereby the symptom and the source of the pain do not match up—so the pain you feel in one part of your body is coming from another part of your body.

I've always had a strange fondness for this fact. Referred pain has an element of mischief. It can't quite be explained. It evades language, racing away from the source just when it is about to be caught. Yet this fondness is misplaced because referred pain can be quite dangerous. The most common presentation of referred pain is when a heart attack appears as a toothache. A patient shows up at the dentist with a toothache, assuming there will be some mildly torturous, wildly expensive, but relatively easy way to heal it. Much to their shock, the patient is not given Novocain but an ambulance ride to the emergency room.

Referred pain is an instance where someone can be both entirely right and entirely wrong about their own lived experience. To say the patient is *wrong* when they go to the dentist because of tooth pain is not quite right. The pain *is* in the jaw. It just didn't start there and can't be healed there either.

As with most things, what happens physically has a correlation psychologically. Referred pain can happen in the psyche too. Sometimes the thing we think is causing the pain is not actually what is causing the pain. This is exactly what was going on with Grace.

Grace showed up with all the classic symptoms of trauma. In fact, when she had gone to a psychiatrist through her employee assistance service at work, she was diagnosed with full-blown PTSD. She was experiencing constant nightmares and intrusive thoughts, had difficulty concentrating, and had noticed a drastically increased startle response. Her sense of self had started to crumble. These shifts in the way that she perceived and moved about in the world led her to conclude that she was losing her mind, that there was something deeply and fundamentally wrong with her. This conclusion spiraled her into a near-complete collapse. She felt intensely guilty for minor mistakes at work and stayed up all night obsessing about every little faux pas with her friends. She spent her free time pacing and pulling her past relationships apart so she could find how *she* had failed. All these symptoms were upsetting and disturbing to her, but the one that was causing the most distress was that she had started to avoid traveling for work—something that she had previously loved to do and found deep meaning in.

The fact that she had these symptoms was not terribly surprising given her work. Grace was a first responder who traveled to disaster sites. She came to me because she found her therapist did not have a lot of knowledge about how the trauma response worked and impacted the brain. She wanted some additional support, education, and practical tools for healing.

I kept having this suspicion that the pain was referred—that the trauma response was *not* the result of her job. Whenever she talked about her job, even the most difficult moments, she *lit up*. She felt effective there; she helped people in meaningful ways. She had a high tolerance for being on site immediately after a disaster struck, and witnessing these perils did not seem to have caused her to believe that the world was unsafe or evil.

All the knowledge I gave her about traumatic experiences resonated with her, but when we tried to apply it to specific work-related situations, the resonating ceased. The nightmares persisted, her startle response remained exaggerated, and she had started to experience some intense gastrointestinal symptoms that got in the way of her ability to work and socialize. The interventions I provided were addressing the pain, but not the source.

One evening during a session, I steered us away from work and back to a recent breakup she had mentioned in passing a couple of times. Each time she had brought it up, she quickly laughed and said, "I certainly don't need to talk about *that*." That night, I asked her why she didn't want to talk about it.

"Well," she said, sighing deeply, "It just really doesn't seem like it should be that important. Certainly not important enough to talk about *here*. It was a two-year relationship for God's sake, not a marriage. I talk to people every day about life-changing tragedies. Yesterday, I spoke to a mother who was trying to come to grips with losing all four of her sons in a terrorist attack. This was just a *fucking breakup*."

Her language was dismissive and casual, but her facial expressions and body language were telling a different story. When she talked about work, she held her head high and her eyes sparkled. She was engaged and dynamic. When she talked about her breakup, she bent inward. Her shoulders slumped and her eyes fixed on her desk. A pallor came over her face, and when she finally lifted her head up to repeat, "just a silly breakup," I saw that her eyes had filled with tears.

Her job was the tooth pain. The breakup was the heart attack.

I started to talk to her about vulnerability. Not just the kind of vulnerability that is involved when we start dating someone new or when we tell someone a secret that we've never shared. The kind of vulnerability that runs like water underneath *everything*.

A part of what it is to be human is to be fundamentally vulnerable, and even worse, to be terribly *aware* of that vulnerability. This vulnerability—the potential to lose anything and everything that we love and hold dear at any moment and for reasons that lie outside of our control—is something that we learn to ignore. We gather our infinite vulnerabilities and stuff them in a glass box, and then we place that glass box on a high shelf. This is not a destructive or inauthentic kind of avoidance. It is survival.

Imagine what life would look like if we faced that vulnerability all the time.

You might wake up in the morning and snuggle up to your partner. Instead of enjoying the warm and loving feeling of that sleepy cuddle, you would feel panic rising in your throat as you thought about how you might not have this opportunity someday—and that someday might be tomorrow. Dwell there long, and you might have a hard time getting out of bed at all. As you jump out of bed to escape the panic, you might trip over your cat, realizing that your beloved pet might not be long for this world and could easily leave it—again, at any moment. Distracted, you bend down to snuggle her up and then quickly realize that if you don't get ready soon, you might be late for work. You love your job, and now you wonder if you might lose it. What would you do then? Why isn't it more secure? Why isn't anything? While rushing in the shower, you might start to lament your aging skin and start to wonder if your health is failing you in invisible ways.

See? The more you notice and dwell on how vulnerable you and the things in your life are, the more you get carried away from the present moment—the moment which is, by the way, slipping away from you right now. Once you take that glass box of infinite vulnerabilities off the shelf and open it, it is difficult to gather up the scattered vulnerabilities and close the box again.

This is one of those maddening contradictions about human life that cannot be reconciled. It makes everything wonderful and terrible, delightful and painful, all at once. The fact that we can lose anything and everything that we love at any moment and for any reason is at the same time an undeniable facet of human existence that we cannot avoid and something we must figure out how to mostly avoid, because if we do not avoid it, we will not be able to live. See? Pain has an element of mischief.

And so, as a brilliant little coping technique, we put that box on a high shelf and unconsciously decide that most things in our daily lives are basically safe to count on and take for granted. This is what it looks like to put the box of infinite vulnerabilities on a high shelf: You enjoy the sleepy cuddle with your partner and take for granted that there will be another opportunity for the same thing tomorrow morning. You trip over the cat and, taking for granted that she will not run into traffic this afternoon, you allow yourself the audacity and grace to even get irritated with her. You get ready for work a little mindlessly, taking your time in the shower and getting ready, not even pausing to consider that you might be a few minutes late.

You take for granted all of this so you can live in the present moment and experience the multitude of emotions that exist other than panic at impending loss. Doing so doesn't negate the fact of our vulnerability, it just makes it possible for us to carry on living alongside it. The vulnerability peeks through every now and again and takes our breath away for a moment, but for the most part, the box of infinite vulnerabilities stays closed, up on the high shelf.

That is until something violent sweeps through and knocks it off, and the box comes crashing to the floor. Suddenly there is glass and vulnerability everywhere, and everything we have been counting on and taking for granted are revealed as they really are: *potential losses*. What will we lose next? How quickly and in what way will we be caught off guard? What will we regret the moment that we realize that it is too late?

This is one of the things about traumatic experiences that make them so uniquely and deeply shattering: The wound does not restrict itself to one spot. It reverberates through *everything*. It stamps our whole life with meaning. We are not just left dealing with the aftermath of the specific traumatic event, but also with the echoing and terrifying truth that the event carries with it—the truth that one vulnerability reveals all vulnerabilities. This truth is infectious, and it quickly spreads through our lives and colors everything with panic and terror. Life can quickly become untenable.

As I explain this to Grace, she starts to cry. She starts talking through her tears.

"We lived together. I've never lived with anyone before. We were looking at houses to buy. We were talking about having babies, getting married. We looked at a beautiful house one Saturday, and the next Saturday, he was driving to Chicago to move in with his new girlfriend. There wasn't even anything wrong. We didn't even have a fight. It was just over—over! Suddenly I was just standing there in the driveway watching him drive away. I still can't understand it, and he never gave me a reason, either. He met someone else online. He is going to take all of the plans that we made together and go live them out with her."

This dude had waltzed out of Grace's life, right out of her present and out of their future. And on his way out he had knocked over her carefully placed box of infinite vulnerabilities, and now there was broken glass and terror all over her life. Worse yet, since Grace didn't think that a "silly breakup" could cause so much damage, she had shamed herself into believing that all the broken glass wasn't even there, even though she walked through it daily.

Grace couldn't go to sleep because her mind was busy trying to make sense of the senselessness. Clearly, she had missed the signs that her relationship was on the rocks and her boyfriend was about to leave. What else might she miss if she stopped pacing? She couldn't eat because she knew on some unconscious level that nourishing herself would be signing on to a future that seemed completely impossible and uninhabitable. She couldn't travel because she didn't think she had an intact life to travel away from and back to. Even the commute to work felt vaguely dangerous. What would happen to her house while she was gone? What might happen to her?

It is *so hard* to move forward in a life where suddenly nothing makes sense.

It's not just the traumatic event that matters—it's also what the traumatic event *means*. In Grace's case, it was not just the traumatic experience that was getting in the way of healing, it was also, in large part, Grace's judgment of it. The shame that she felt for being this upset over a breakup was sitting like a boulder in the middle of her path. This judgment and shame was not born in a vacuum, it was sponsored and made possible by societal opinion and judgment.

Instead of noticing that the pain was referred and trying to treat it at the source, Grace was judging herself for the pain. Based on a deeply problematic societal understanding of trauma, she had decided this particular loss simply did not count. She did not have the luxury of feeling this way about this loss because "It was silly," and "It was only a two-year relationship," and "There are bigger traumas out there. I see that every day."

I told her three very important things.

1. Neither love nor loss are ever silly.

2. It might have only been a two-year relationship, but it was a two-year relationship with a very detailed happily-ever-after built into it. When we mourn, we are tasked with mourning not only the loss of someone, but also the future we had planned with them. We encounter that future in unanticipated ways, and so the task of mourning continues to roll out in front of us.

3. The presence of "bigger traumas" doesn't negate the existence of "little traumas." In fact, this distinction doesn't make sense at all.

Let's talk more about number 3.

BIG-T TRAUMA, LITTLE-T TRAUMA

The distinction between capital-T and lowercase-T trauma, like much of the language around traumatic experience, came from a real clinician and has a real purpose—one that has been *completely and entirely* left behind.

Francine Shapiro developed Eye Movement Desensitization and Reprocessing (EMDR) in 1987. At the time, there was no clinical distinction between types of traumatic experience. The DSM defined a traumatic stressor as any experience that was "generally outside the range of usual human experience and that would evoke significant distress symptoms in almost everyone."[1] The primary feature of traumatic experience was its uniqueness, the fact that it stood just outside of normal.

Shapiro found that EMDR, the mechanics of which I will get into below, was indeed a helpful tool for people who had experienced things that were "generally outside the range of usual human experience." It helped them recalibrate after the abnormal had scrambled their sense of the world. But she also suspected the EMDR protocol would be helpful for experiences that evoked significant stress in many people but were not outside the range of usual human experience. Childhood humiliations and disappointments, for example, would not be clinically recognized as traumatic events as they unfortunately fall entirely within the range of usual human experience. But, they might leave "comparable, lasting negative effects" that could erode one's sense of self and trust in the external world. Shapiro found that the effects of these more quotidian traumas could be mitigated by using EMDR even though the nature of the stressor would not qualify as traumatic from a clinical perspective. If EMDR was restricted to people who had experienced a stressor that counted as traumatic clinically, those who were suffering similarly, but for different reasons, would miss out.

To lend legitimacy to the experiences that were not being accounted for in trauma studies without having to challenge the DSM and the entire psychiatric institution behind it, Shapiro coined the term "small-t traumatic events." This was *not* an attempt to create a hierarchical distinction between two kinds of traumatic events. In fact, it was quite the opposite. She was claiming that these two kinds of events are nearly neurobiologically *identical*, which is why the negative effects of both could be successfully treated by EMDR.

When Shapiro introduced this distinction between small-T and large-T traumatic events, she was simply trying to level the playing field—to remove some of the judgment so the intervention she had built could be applied wherever it might be effective. Though the language of small-T and big-T trauma comes from a very legitimate place, this does not guarantee its current use is legitimate. Because of our penchant for categories, distinctions, and hierarchies, this language has been co-opted and used to shame us.

How this legitimate and intentional terminology became co-opted and twisted is unclear. I hear the phrases "uppercase and lowercase trauma" or "capital-T and lowercase-T trauma" often, and they are never used to make someone's experience *more* legitimate. Typically, someone is calling their own traumatic experience "lowercase" to make sure whoever is listening knows they are aware that other people have it worse. Or someone is calling their own experience "uppercase" in order to explain how their struggles are legitimate compared to their partner, who only experienced trauma in the "lowercase."

This perceived distinction between people's experiences reveals a much bigger problem with the way that trauma is defined clinically. The clinical world has been trying to define trauma by beginning at the *type* of event rather than the *way* the event is experienced. This means we begin the study of traumatic experience with a judgment. When someone shows the symptoms of a stuck trauma response, but the stressor they were exposed to (bullying at work, for example) does not pass muster for the definition of a traumatic event, we do not turn and question the *definition*. We instead question the *person suffering*. If the stressor doesn't fit our definition, their symptoms *must* be a result of their own weakness, pathology, or lack of resilience.

This distinction not only causes problems for events that supposedly do not count as traumatic, but it also causes problems for events that *do* count as traumatic according to the DSM. Two combat soldiers who go through the very same deployment can experience it in radically different ways. One may come home and struggle with PTSD for years, while the other may reintegrate successfully and quickly without struggle. Here we might blame the one who struggles, holding up his comrade for comparison: "Well, he seemed to do okay. Do you have any other underlying issues with anxiety? No? Hmm. Well, is it possible that you're using this so-called PTSD to get out of something?" We might also blame the one who does not struggle, suspiciously questioning whether he really is doing okay: "Trauma is very common for people deployed in that part of Afghanistan. In fact, some of your brigade members are suffering deeply. Are you sure you're not numbing with alcohol?" When we begin our inquiry with a judgment, it stops being an inquiry at all.

It's important to recognize how deeply language shapes our inner experience. This is part of the reason why Grace cannot recognize her own lasting trauma response. It is why she spent months having repetitive nightmares and not being able to eat. It is why she found herself retching into a trash can in the subway station one morning on her way to work. It is why she spent several weeks considering leaving her meaningful job because she thought it *must* be the thing causing these symptoms.

When we try to compare our traumatic experiences with another's, when we create hierarchies and categories, we do far more harm than good. After all, the trauma response is rooted in the amygdala, which is a part of your brain not sophisticated enough to distinguish between capital and lowercase traumas at all. The amygdala is too primitive to even learn the alphabet. To this part of you, threat is threat is threat and trauma is trauma is trauma. Asking this part of your brain to tell the difference between big and small trauma is like asking the smoke alarm in your kitchen to differentiate between smoke from cooking bacon and the smoke of a house fire. *Not* gonna happen.

The question to ask is not whether someone *else* would think that your experience qualified as traumatic, but whether it was traumatic for *you*. If you're not sure, take a look at the things you are counting on and taking for granted. Are they intact? Are you able to keep the understanding that we are infinitely vulnerable at arm's length and be present in your daily life? Or did the box of infinite vulnerability fall off the high shelf and shatter, leaving your life strewn with broken glass and abject terror?

This question is only the beginning. The realization that Grace's pain was referred—that her trauma response had been activated by the event *she* experienced as traumatic rather than the event someone else would pick out as potentially traumatic—was just the beginning. Now that we had found the source, we had to figure out what to do about it.

Often, in order to put the box of infinite vulnerabilities back up on its high shelf, we have to remind our poor little bodies that being terrified all the time does not actually help. We can do this by recalibrating our nervous system.

TRAUMA AND TOP-DOWN REGULATION

Most disruptive symptoms of the trauma response are rooted in memory. As you may remember from chapter 3, the brain's alarm system codes certain pieces from the overwhelming experience as inherently threatening. When something in our internal or external environment brings one or more of those pieces forward into our consciousness, the brain's alarm is tripped, and the nervous system is off to the races.

This response can be problematic in lots of ways. One is that you cannot just put the box of infinite vulnerabilities back on the shelf and go about the business of enjoying your life. When your stress response system is in overdrive all the time, it becomes really easy to clue in to all the potential ways the world is dangerous and completely miss what is going on in the present moment. We become fixated on the infinite vulnerabilities and dwell on potential loss, potential pain, and potential horror. That terror robs us of our present by mashing together problems from our past and our fears for the future, which metastasize when we live from our amygdalae.

To heal your trauma and stop you from feeling this way, your memory needs some organization and refiling. To quickly review, each long-term memory file contains three things: a coherent narrative of the event, emotional content from the event, and a label (or a few labels) assigning meaning. When a file is organized and well-integrated, you can find it when you need to, flip through the contents, and put it back—all with relative ease.

For example, if I were to ask you what your wedding day was like, you might start with some of the emotional content, such as, "It was the most beautiful and exciting day." As you review that emotional content, you likely feel some of those emotions because that's how this kind of memory works. As you talk about that day, you smile and feel a warm glow in the center of your chest. Then you might dip into the narrative content and give me a basic chronology of the day, about what it was like to plan and how you got ready with all of your bridesmaids and took silly photos while you did your makeup together. You might stumble upon a funny memory you hadn't thought about in a while and laugh. Then a moment later, you might tell me about a really moving toast given by someone who has since died.

At any point in this process, if something else came up that called for your attention, you could set the file down and tend to the interruption. For example, if in the midst of telling the story your toddler came into the room and asked for a snack, you could switch gears easily. You could have a conversation with them about what kind of snack they wanted, make that snack, help them eat it, and send them back to the playroom. This is a sign that the memory is well integrated: you can engage with it and then put it away when you need to.

Another sign of an integrated memory is that it has a set of tags or labels that assign it meaning in the larger arc of your narrative self. If I asked you what the memory of that day meant to you, you might label it as: *the best day of my life, the beginning of a very long road, the best decision I've ever made.* Those are the tags or labels on the file. What this memory means to you is as important as the content in the file. The files can also change over time. If your marriage suddenly ended, you might retag that file with different labels: *the most naïve decision I ever made, the beginning of the end, an event I would really like to have a second chance at.*

Most of our memories look more or less like this, and most of our memories are more or less integrated. One of the central features of traumatic memories is that they do not look like this and are not integrated. This is a problem not just for our memory, for our neat little folders and file cabinets, but for our entire nervous system because the memory fragments, which are sharp and jagged, are recognized by the alarm system as a threat.

And as we know, when your brain recognizes a threat, it sets off the stress response system. This system reprioritizes the normal processes in your body to help you prepare for the threat so you will be more likely to respond effectively and stay alive. This response is great when you are being chased by a wolf, or when the smoke alarm in your house goes off in the middle of the night because faulty wiring in the kitchen has sparked a fire behind the wall. It is not so great when the brain reacts to something innocuous because it brings up a disorganized memory file and all the disruptive emotions and responses that go with it while you are just trying to get through the workday.

Again, this response happens for a very good reason and indicates that your alarm is working. Just because the smoke alarm goes off when you are making bacon doesn't mean it isn't working. But when the alarm goes off at innocuous stimuli, this means the alarm has gotten a bit over-sensitive and could use some recalibration. One of the ways we can start recalibrating the stress response system is by working against the reprioritization of physical functions that begins when the brain detects threat.

When the amygdala sets off the alarm system in the brain, blood flow and electrical activity pull away from the prefrontal cortex (which is in charge of lots of things, but chief among them is rational thought and working memory) and the hippocampus (the good ole file cabinet). This can be a huge problem when you're trying to access a traumatic memory so that you can think rationally about it in order to change its meaning tags and reorder the narrative. When the alarm system goes off you don't actually get any retelling work done, you just get re-exposed to the trauma response continually. Your system is operating under the assumption that you are, still or once again, in clear and present danger.

When blood flow and electrical activity are being pulled away from the brain structures that we need to work on the traumatic memory, we have to manually intervene and send some of that blood flow and electrical activity back to other parts of the brain (specifically, the prefrontal cortex and the hippocampus). This redirection will slow down the stress response system, which will make the body feel calm instead of amped.

When we use the top of our brain to regulate our system all the way down to our toes, we are using *top-down regulation*.

Top-down regulation is one of the reasons why EMDR is an effective means of addressing traumatic memories. During an EMDR session, the practitioner begins by engaging your working memory (which is in your prefrontal cortex). They do this by giving you a task that requires your concentration and your visual field. This task can vary, but typically you are asked to follow a beam of light or a moving object back and forth with your eyes. While your working memory is online and your prefrontal cortex has blood flow and electrical activity, you can access the traumatic memory and start to sort through the disorganized file with the practitioner. When the alarm system starts to go off, as it invariably will, your prefrontal cortex can step in and use rational thought to recognize that the threat is not current. Over time, your brain is more likely to recognize the content from the memory file as neutral and nonthreatening, and you can do the necessary work to integrate the memory file.

It is important to understand that this process does not erase the emotional content in the memory file. Nothing can do that. But it does change the *intensity* of the emotional content because the brain no longer thinks the emotional content is going to kill you. Traumatic memories are never going to become happy or neutral memories. They will still have emotional content, and the emotional content might cause you to cry or feel anxious for a few minutes. The difference is that they will no longer hijack your entire day. You will be able to see the traumatic experience as an event in your life—like all the other events in your life—and you will feel empowered to add your own meaning to it.

If your goal for trauma healing is to stop feeling entirely, you are setting yourself up for failure. If I tell you about the morning my father died, I will likely tear up. I might feel the gray and cloudy grief start to take up space in my lungs. This memory still has emotional content, but it long ago stopped being the kind of memory that wakes me up in the middle of the night in a panic.

Grace underwent EMDR and talked about the day that her boy-friend left. She talked about all of the losses involved in their split, and that she now felt infinitely vulnerable in a way that made her trip over every minute of every day. Over time, she stopped having nightmares. She was able to eat, go to work, and even date again. She still sometimes thinks about the infinite vulnerabilities, but for the most part, they are on the high shelf, safe in a brand-new glass box.

TAKEAWAYS AND TOOLS

When we assume the trauma response is a sign of weakness or dysfunction, we also often assume that to have lasting traces of trauma—be it a full-blown diagnosis of PTSD or just a life spent grappling with some of the symptoms—means we have been broken in a way that cannot be fixed. We assume the traumatic event and trauma response have changed us, that we will always be like this, that we will never come back to calm. I know this because I believed it about my own experience for a very long time.

It's bullshit.

Traumatic symptoms are the result of our natural adaptive systems becoming maladaptive over time. The alarm system adapts and goes off, and then it can't stop going off. However, the fact that our systems are malleable means that, though it can be very difficult, it is totally within our capacity to change their course. Let me give you an example.

Since I am in the higher education and mental health fields, I am an essential worker and did not experience a pause in either of my jobs during the pandemic. But the shutdown greatly impacted my time outside of work. I remember sitting in my apartment on a Saturday afternoon in March 2020, a few days after the shutdown began as a protective measure against COVID-19. I was as anxious as a baby bird and nothing I would normally do in times of stress was available to me. Stores and coffee shops were closed. Yoga studios and gyms were closed. Even the hiking trails and parks near me were closed.

"Well," I thought, glancing a little frantically around for something to do, "I'm not going to be able to do this."

I needed not only something to do, but also a little bit of joy. So I went on the Target website and ordered some colored pencils, a coloring book, and some candy. As the pandemic and the shutdown went on, the coloring book turned into some embroidery hoops and thread, a sewing machine, and a boxing bag and gloves. I worked, wrote, watched everything on Netflix and then Hulu, downloaded TikTok, made cookies, listened to every podcast on the planet, and went along gathering hobbies. Most of them I never would have otherwise tried, and many of them have stuck.

While, of course, there were many people who did not have the privilege, luxury, or energy to go hobby shopping, those who did, did so voraciously. Collectively, we baked so much bread that there was a run on yeast. We planted roses and vegetables, learned new musical instruments and languages, walked and hiked, bought bikes, and tried CrossFit and HIIT workouts in our driveways. We learned to dance salsa in the backyard. We tried watercolor painting and sculpting with clay and completed massive puzzles on our living room floors.

Some of us even made a hobby out of harshly judging people's hobbies. We wrote think pieces about how baking was yet another disgusting proof of privilege and dancing was cultural appropriation. We posted on social media about how those complicated ombré puzzles with just color and no picture were not accessible to those with colorblindness and how dare we. Angrily missing the point entirely and then writing a Medium article about it can be a hobby too. When we collapse into shaming each other and ourselves, we overlook the astounding miracle of our natural response to overwhelm and the often-brilliant coping tools we reach for without realizing how much we need them and why they work so well.

Each of those hobbies—especially if they are new and unfamiliar—requires input from the working memory. When we are under threat, intentionally switching on this part of the brain—which does not require immediate action—is a way to restore relative homeostasis to the brain. In addition, many of the hobbies provide a way to complete the stress cycle that gets kickstarted when we wake up to catastrophic headlines informing us of more deaths, virus variants, political unrest, shootings, and economic downfall.

The coolest part? We collectively reached for these things during a time of unprecedented trauma and stress without consciously knowing what we were doing. We did so naturally.

We so often focus on coping techniques that arise from necessity and are eventually harmful—alcohol and substances to numb overwhelming emotions, for example. Unhealthy coping mechanisms are no doubt a worthy topic, especially as we find ourselves in the midst of an opioid epidemic that has nearly decimated an entire generation. But if we could forgive ourselves for the self-destructive or unhealthy things we reached for during overwhelm, more of us could heal.

And if we could engage in less judgment and less shame, and make a commitment to bring light into the darkness without those things, we would be a whole lot better at recognizing where the pain is coming from. The more people who know that a heart attack can mask itself as jaw pain, the less people must needlessly die from cardiac arrest. And the more people who know that it is not the type of event but the way that the event is *experienced* that causes trauma, the more likely it is that we will be able to recover from traumatic experiences.

TRAUMA TOOL: TETRIS

If reading about EMDR has sent you googling for a practitioner, lean into that interest. It is a well-respected and scientifically verified intervention that has very little in the way of negative side effects. It might also be helpful to know the theoretical basis of EMDR is the reason I'm suggesting you add the old-school videogame Tetris to your toolbox of things you can use outside the therapist's office.

Yes, you read that correctly: playing Tetris on your phone is a therapeutic tool.

Several studies have shown Tetris to be an effective adjunctive therapy for PTSD. It can mitigate intrusive memories and thoughts, potentially help prevent the development of PTSD after a traumatic event, and even increase hippocampal volume in those who suffer from PTSD. Studies suggest that playing the game for twenty to sixty minutes a day can lower your baseline anxiety level.[2]

You can reach for Tetris any time you are feeling anxious or activated at the wrong moment—meaning, a moment when there is no actual threat or a moment when there is a threat that is not immediate but your body thinks it is (such as when you read the news and encounter real threats you cannot do anything about). The reason it works is the same reason that EMDR is so effective: When the game makes a demand on your visual-spatial system, which is in your prefrontal cortex, blood flow and electrical activity are forced into that area of your brain and away from the alarm system. This effectively turns the alarm system off, sending a message that whatever has been detected as a threat is a false alarm. Over time, the alarm system becomes recalibrated—less sensitized—and learns to go off only when there is an actual threat and to shut down more quickly when the alarm is a false one. Shelf, meet box.

Any other activity that makes a demand on your prefrontal cortex would also work. You just need to be *mindful* of what you are engaging with and how. For example, looking at social media can be a great tool for reengaging your prefrontal cortex, but not if you use it to compare your life with others and wind up feeling insecure. Or if you look up your exes and revisit moments of embarrassment and rejection. Or if you fight with folks whose political leanings do not match up with yours. Or if you respond to colleagues and friends out of obligation. When I want to use social media to engage my prefrontal cortex, I look at bunnies on Instagram. And sometimes baby goats.

In general, notice how you feel doing different activities and let that be your guide. If the activity is making you feel angry, upset, or nervous, it means your amygdala is online and pulling resources from the prefrontal cortex. If the activity is making you feel peaceful and is requiring some focus, it means your prefrontal cortex is online and pulling resources back from the amygdala.

CHAPTER 5

Max's Hourglass

When Loss Is Traumatic

> Nothing can make up for the absence of someone whom we
> love, and it would be wrong to try to find a substitute; we must
> simply hold out and see it through. That sounds very hard at
> first, but at the same time it is a great consolation, for the gap, as
> long as it remains unfilled, preserves the bonds between us.

Dietrich Bonhoeffer

Max hasn't stopped talking since I started the clock for our session. It's been twenty-two minutes, and she hasn't paused once—not to exchange niceties, not to take a breath, not to check in or ask a question.

"And then the last thing I didn't tell you yet is that I'm pregnant. Pregnant! I made an appointment, though, because of course I'm not having it. You know, I keep thinking of an hourglass. Every time I close my eyes, I picture an hourglass. Except the sand isn't going slow. It's moving down *fast*. Faster and faster. And faster. Anyway, the point of all of this is that I just need someone who I can tell everything to, you know? Maybe that will slow the sand. I never tell anyone *everything*. It's too much. Too much to carry. It's too much for *me*. How could anyone else possibly handle it? But time is racing away, and I'm losing track and

I just don't know. Nothing makes any sense. So . . . do you think you can help?"

I feel a bit as if Max has just tossed a giant, gnarled up ball of yarn to me and said, "Here—this is my little life. If we can't get it sorted fast, I can't go on. Help!" I'm pretty sure I didn't even catch all the storylines. Something about a big move, a scandal at work, a relationship-ending fight with her mother, the death of a friend, a divorce, and a pregnancy. It came at me so quickly that it felt like the plot of a telenovela—racing and irrational.

For some reason as she was talking, my mind got stuck on the hourglass image.

"This might seem a little random, but I want you to travel with me just for a minute," I tell her. "We'll make a plan and start sorting things out, but I want to tell you about sawdust art first."

"Sawdust art?" Max looks pretty surprised, maybe a little annoyed.

"Yeah, I know. My students sometimes tell me that I'm the most random person they know. It will connect, I promise. Infiorata festivals take place in Italy in June every year. All night long, artists build intricate and beautiful carpets along the street using colored sawdust (they used to use flowers, but these days most of the displays are laid out with colored sawdust). They use little sifters and filters and stencils and paintbrushes, and they make this art that is more stunning than I can possibly describe, and they make it right there in the middle of the street. It's bright, complex, hard to believe. They stay up all night, and it's set up so you can walk around and watch as they create. The cafés stay open too. Nobody goes to sleep.

"Then, as soon as the sun comes up in the morning and all the sawdust paintings are done, a mass marches right through them, sending the oh-so-carefully placed sawdust flying. And just like that, all that painstaking beauty is gone. *Poof!*

"I think about this sawdust art all the time because, to me, sometimes all of life feels like that—vivid, breathtaking, transient. Sometimes I can appreciate that and be in awe of it, and sometimes I'm really frustrated and heartbroken by it. It's hard not to see everything as being just about to disappear, you know?"

While I'm talking, Max sits back in her chair. Her shoulders relax. She is finally taking a breath. As soon as the question mark comes out of my mouth, she leans forward and starts racing again. Her whole affect races.

"Yes! I do know. I do know that. That's exactly it. Except I feel like my painting isn't going to get done in time. It's like the mass is going to come marching through and I won't be done, and so I'll be saying, 'Wait! Wait! Let me just have a few more minutes, I haven't figured it all out yet! The morning came too fast!'"

I recognize this racing *so very well*. Although Max has several problems that don't seem to relate to each other at all, I am willing to bet that the main source of distress is the death of her friend. I'll bet this loss hit Max like a bomb, and all the rest of these bits are leftover shrapnel she keeps finding scattered all over her body.

You know how in action movies after some big explosion, the main character is sent reeling backward onto the concrete and left with ringing ears and wobbly vision? That's where Max is. Only she's stuck there. So the movie is going on without her, and she hasn't landed back into her body yet. The traumatic loss detonated and *everything* stopped making sense.

THE INEVITABILITY OF TRAUMATIC LOSS

Loss is a guarantee for all of us. Part of being human involves living through loss. Sometimes those losses are things we have time to prepare for. Grandparents die after long illnesses, but we have time to say goodbye. We are all sad, but there is peace, and we gladly accept it. But sometimes losses are not things we can prepare for. They are sudden. Wrenching. Unfair. *Unthinkable*. Some of us will have entire *lists* of these kinds of losses by the time we're adults. But the fact that they are common does not make them easy.

When I was in graduate school, a close friend died suddenly. I found out on my way to class and my professor found me sitting in the hallway outside the classroom, ashen and open-mouthed. He told me to go home and said he'd share the notes from the lecture with me. I nodded and started getting my things together. Before he went back into the classroom, he told me to read Ralph Waldo Emerson's essay "Experience."

"Just trust me. It'll help," he said. "In fact, you can present on it for us next week. That way I know you'll read it."

Stunned and red-eyed, I made my way home and let the shock waves run through me while I sat on the train. All I could think about was my friend's laugh—gravelly, easy, contagious. I'd never hear it again. It already felt like it was slipping away. Gravelly, easy . . . Wait, what was the third thing? Dizzy with shock, I sat at my little kitchen table and opened Emerson's *Essays and Lectures*, looking for "Experience."

Emerson is notorious for being nearly impossible to crack, and this essay was no exception. It begins, "Where do we find ourselves? In a series of which we do not know the extremes, and believe that it has none. We wake and find ourselves on a stair; there are stairs below us, which we seem to have ascended; there are stairs above us, many a one, which go upward and out of sight."[1] And on the first, and second, and fifth, and seventh read, those were just about the only sentences in the whole essay that I could follow. My professor seemed to think this essay was going to help me understand the loss of my friend, but the essay felt hollowed out, cold, eerie. When I read it, I felt like I was there on that staircase, confused at how I got there and where I was going. I needed some context. If I couldn't figure out *what* Emerson meant, maybe it would help if I knew *why* he wrote it. So I went to his journals.

January 28, 1842: "Yesterday night, at fifteen minutes after eight, my little Waldo ended his life."[2] It's the only sentence on the page; the rest was blank. It took my breath away.

There was the context: loss. Emerson's son Waldo had died at the age of five of scarlet fever. Waldo, who was "my little Waldo." Waldo, of whom Emerson wrote, "I have seen the poor boy, when he came to a tuft of violets in the wood, kneel down on the ground, smell of them, kiss them, and depart without plucking them."[3] Waldo, who "gave up his little innocent breath like a bird."[4]

Emerson was writing grief. He wasn't writing *about* grief; he was *writing grief*.

The pieces of the essay started to shift and make sense. In one puzzling sentence that had gotten stuck and rolled around in my head, Emerson remarks that the most unhandsome part of the human condition is "the evanescence and lubricity of all objects, which lets them slip through our fingers then when we clutch hardest."[5] As I looked at that passage through the lens of grief, its meaning became clearer: The most unfortunate part of being human is that we have this tendency to grasp, even though everything we grasp will slip through our fingers. We are made to grasp, and the world is made to slip away.

Ouch.

This sentence made me think of a beautiful line in *The Empathy Exams*, where Leslie Jamison writes, "A root system of loss stretches radial and rhyzomatic under the entire territory of my life."[6] She is writing of her own experience, but it is true for all of us, all the time. We are all held up by root systems of loss. And if that's true, that other people are always slipping away from us, it must be the case that we are also slipping away. In our losing, we are also being lost. No wonder Max is thinking about an hourglass. No wonder the sand seems to be moving too fast for her.

Though it may sound like a contradiction, it is this root system of loss that defines our connections with one another and makes them possible.

My professor had given me that assignment because he recognized I had just awoken on Emerson's staircase for the first time and he wanted me to know I wasn't alone. I was supposed to be on the staircase. And what I was struggling with was something we all struggle with—something we've *always* been struggling with.

Over the course of five or six sessions, Max starts to slow down and tell me more about what's been going on. The friend who died was a dear one, a boy named Paul who Max met in the fourth grade. Their relationship had some drama right from the start. A year after meeting and becoming best friends, Paul moved away. Max was devastated. She wrote about Paul in her little pink journal with a lock. How she thought she might love him. How mad she was at his dad for taking that job two states away. How she'd never get over the loss and never love anyone as deeply. Two years later, against all odds, Paul moved back.

"When have you *ever* heard of that happening?" asks Max. As she leans forward for emphasis, I see her as a sixth grader, asking her mom the very same question at the dining room table.

I think, but don't say: Never. I've heard lots of stories of people reuniting after years and years, meeting up again at a high school reunion after two divorces and five kids, or finding each other on social media after the death of their spouses. But I've never heard of a kid getting to move back to his friend two years after he moved away.

They had remained friends for seventeen years, right up until the morning Paul went out for a run and never came home. For a few days, he was missing. There were search parties and Facebook posts. And then he was identified—in the city morgue. He had fallen and hit his head and died instantly. At twenty-eight.

Unthinkable.

Faced with the slipping away of her very best friend, Max had started slipping away too. She had an affair with a colleague—a dangerous one that could have cost her both her marriage and her job. Then, on a whim, she traded one job for another and moved. She became deeply embroiled with a scandal at work. Got divorced. Started dating again. Fell in love. Got pregnant. Started cheating again.

One day during a session, Max folded over and put her head in her hands. She looked absolutely tortured. She didn't make sense to herself.

"I don't even *want* to be doing this shit. What the *fuck* is wrong with me?"

"Well, Max, it seems to me like you're hedging. Rehearsing loss. You're afraid to lean into any one thing, so you're scattering yourself over the country, over a couple of different jobs, over a handful of relationships. There's something in you that seems driven to scatter like this, as if it'll be some kind of insurance, some kind of guarantee. If you're nowhere, you can't be lost. If you've committed to nothing, you can't lose."

She looks at me, ashen and open-mouthed. "That's it. That's it." She starts to cry.

Max feels alone in this loss, and in a way she is. She has made herself alone in it. She has scattered herself so far and wide that she can't even gather herself up again. But she's also not at all alone in it. We're all up against this white whale. Once we face any kind of loss at all, our connections become ridden with potential loss. Some of us are more capable of ignoring it, but it's there whether we want to admit it or not.

TRAUMATIC LOSS AND THE BRAIN

At this point you might be wondering what loss like this has to do with the brain or the trauma response. The answer is everything. Loss is potentially traumatic, but we sometimes don't label it as such. I suspect the reason why is rooted in an old definition. Remember, in the DSM trauma was defined as "that which lay outside the norm." Because losses are inevitable, because we will all face many of them—some expected, some shocking—we are inclined to label them as "not traumatic." Or we distinguish between those types of losses that might be traumatic and those that simply cannot be.

But remember what we are learning (and unlearning) about traumas: traumatic experience should not be defined in terms of *what* happened, but in terms of the *reaction* the experience causes. When an experience overwhelms the nervous system to the point that our emergency trauma response kicks into gear and switches off our recording and filing processes, it is *potentially* traumatic. When we can't calm and reset our systems, and we can't find someone to help us find the off switch for the trauma response, that experience becomes *lastingly traumatic*. So just because loss is something we all face does not mean that a loss can't be traumatic. Further, which losses will be traumatic and which will not be is not something we can predict. For example, an expected loss after someone has had a long life and a prolonged illness can be traumatic if you've tied your identity to the role of caretaker for that person and don't have a good support system in your grief.

All hierarchies of loss, like hierarchies of traumatic experience, are built in shame.

The loss that Max suffered when she lost her friend was a traumatic one. It overwhelmed her system and shut off her recording mechanisms. So instead of the loss becoming an integrated and meaningful memory, she's dealing with a trauma response that won't shut off. And the way that it's showing up is a little sneaky. Instead of nightmares and a heightened startle response, she's engaging in behaviors that ensure she does not connect with others and therefore can never lose someone again. Since our coping mechanisms are often designed by our more primitive brain structure (the amygdala), they are not rational and can lead to behavior that feels compulsive and driven by fear. So while these mechanisms aim to protect us, they ultimately undermine us. This is probably why Max feels like time is racing. It's because she's not choosing her next move—fear is. Max's chronically activated emergency systems have tricked her into thinking that connection equals danger, and so behaviorally, she is trying to trick the system. Scatter yourself over as many superficial connections as possible and you'll never be vulnerable to loss.

Just like trauma that comes from any other source, this trauma needs to be integrated in order for Max to be able to change her behavior. To integrate it, she first has to face it. So over many sessions, I help her do just that. We sit down with the memory file that contains her relationship with her friend and the repeated loss of him—first in fourth grade and again when he died. She feels the emotional content that is there. We talk about what those losses meant and how they shaped her. Once we faced the thing that was sending Max scattered all over the country and across several relationships, she stopped racing. Time started to slow and she started to commit to things that she wanted. She is still scared of loss, but now that fear shows up almost as a kind of reverence rather than a destructive force—an indication of how much something or someone means to her.

TAKEAWAYS AND TOOLS

In *The Work of Mourning*, Jacques Derrida writes, "To have a friend, to look at him, to follow him with your eyes, to admire him in friendship, is to know in a more intense way, already injured, always insistent, and more and more unforgettable, that one of the two of you will inevitably see the other die."[7]

Again, ouch.

All of our relationships are marked with inevitable loss. It looms large on the horizon, an ever-present specter. And yet it is also already here. At the very moment we connect, we already begin slipping away. Our relationships are comprised of—indeed, constituted by—becoming entangled and then slipping away.

When we connect with one another, there is a kind of reaching out. I tell you something about myself; I show you something of mine. But what I give you—a thought, a secret, a hug—recedes as soon as it is given. Then I ask something of you: What do you think? How do you feel? What do you like? Just like that, we are stuck. We do not need death to lose one other. We are slipping away from each other all the time.

So here we are. What it means to be human is to be transient and to be surrounded by transience (just like the sawdust paintings). We desire and we come undone. We grasp and then we lose. We become entangled and then we slip away. We learn the lesson and then we make the mistake all over again.

But is it a mistake? Once we know loss, why do we submit to it over and over again? I ask myself this question a lot. Because it is our job to struggle with this question. This is what it means to be human. And the goal is not to avoid loss (we can't), but to try and not get too stuck on the grasping or the grieving.

TRAUMA TOOL: WHAT REMAINS

I've always found the rituals around death to be oddly comforting—the careful way we tend to the remains of a person, how gently we lay them to rest. We aren't the only species to engage in these gentle and holy rituals. Elephants touch the bones of their dead gently with their trunks, cover the body with leaves and dirt, and sit with the deceased for weeks at a time.

But remains aren't just the body of the deceased. Remains also refer to what endures after death. When we ask what remains of a life, we are asking, what endures, what abides, what lasts? This may seem like an offensive question. You might want to resist it initially. Your answer might be, "Nothing. *Nothing* endures." That's okay. Leave it be and come back in a few weeks.

When my father died, there were so many sympathy cards that it took weeks to get through them and months to write thank-you notes back. Many of these cards were a testament to what remained of my father even in his stunning absence.

One of the letters was from a man who'd had my father as a dentist when he was a child. He wrote:

> My family and I send our deepest sympathies to you and your family. We're deeply saddened by Bob's passing, and I find myself thinking of him very often.
>
> Most twelve-year-old children didn't have the relationship that I had with my dentist. That was the year that I spent about one day a week for approximately twenty-five weeks undergoing root canals. Although most would cringe at the thought, I would always look forward to getting into that chair. He always had a kind word and a genuine smile. He was truly a gentle soul.
>
> I'm not sure if you were all aware of it but things were very difficult for me at home. His kind presence was so soothing and made such a lasting impression on me that in a way I feel it saved me from perpetuating the abuse that I grew up with. Although I could not have a father like him, I often imagined what it would be like. Those imaginings formed the basis of how I am as a father now.
>
> I am just sad to know that I was never able to express to Bob how much his kindness meant. He was truly an extraordinary man, doing angelic things here on earth. Not only was he fixing smiles, but in his own quiet way and perhaps without even realizing it, he was mending hearts as well.
>
> I miss him and will always remember him.

I don't know what I believe about the afterlife, and I probably never will, but this letter showed me that, in a very real and tangible way, my father's spirit lived on. This hint of what remained helped me to see that there were many things I got to keep, that the loss wasn't the whole story.

For this exercise, you'll need to put down the never-ending list of what's been lost. Don't worry, you won't ever lose that list. You can return to it as soon as you're done here. But if you are only looking at that list, you're missing what remains, what endures, what abides, and what lasts.

> **Step 1:** For a few minutes, bring to mind the loved one you lost. Think of all your favorite things about them.

> **Step 2:** Start making a list of what you get to keep even though they are gone. Funny memories? Their sense of humor? The lesson they taught you in fourth grade about how to do long division?

> **Step 3:** Think of three to five concrete ways that you can carry these things forward into your life. Can you teach other people that same lesson? Make sure to be generous in the same way they were? Tell everyone you can their favorite joke?

Making this list is not a way to negate what you've lost; it's a way to embrace it more entirely. And it's not a way to negate everything that has gone missing. Trust me, I know just how long that list is and how excruciatingly real its contents are. The point is to gently remind yourself that loss is not all there is, that the world is not all horror, that even in the most shattering losses, *something* remains.

CHAPTER 6

Erica's Trauma Bond
Why We Reenact Traumatizing Patterns

There's a dark side to each and every human soul. We wanna be Obi-Wan
Kenobi, and for the most part we are, but there's a little Darth Vader
in all of us. [. . .] My experience? Face the darkness. Stare it down and
own it. It's like brother Nietzsche said, being human is a complicated
gig, so give that ol' dark night of the soul a hug and howl the eternal yes.

Chris Stevens (played by John Corbett) in *Northern Exposure*

I've just finished writing a statement to the court for Erica. I'm writing
as her and begging for jail time and an extension of a restraining order
against her ex-husband, who is actively trying to kill her. These are
things that nobody should have to beg for. I'm writing it in her voice
because her relationship tore her voice away.

I'm explaining for her that sometimes our behavior becomes inexplicable to ourselves. Sometimes we keep in touch with people who have
tried to annihilate us because not to do so is unthinkable, impossible.
As it turns out, trying to reconcile two completely different and coun-
terposed versions of a person is a very big and difficult task. Version A is
a person who charmed you, a person you trusted, laughed with, fell in
love with, and married. Version B is a person who behaves like a mon-
ster; a person who finds your weakest points and takes you out by deftly

launching an arrow right to the center; a person who puts their hands on you, not lovingly, but violently; a person whose other version gets lost in their suddenly black irises. These two versions are so distant from one other that they seem like two different people, two people who might even have different mannerisms and facial expressions. But in an act defying reason, making reason fold in on itself and collapse into doubt, these two people share a body and have the same face.

You can see how things quickly stop making sense.

Erica tripped up exactly *once*. She wrote a letter to her ex-husband on the day of their wedding anniversary and told him how she was feeling about the disintegration of their life together. She didn't ask for a response or ask him any questions. She just explained how she was feeling. He reached out, apologized for absolutely everything, and told her he was entering a program to help with his anger issues. She began to hope that maybe there were *not* two contradictory people in one man. Maybe she was wrong. Maybe this kind of shattering and staggering experience wasn't real.

Four days later, he came to her house and tried to kill her.

Since she is the one who reached out, the only explanation that the court will entertain is that she is and always has been a manipulative liar. She must not *really* be afraid of him if she emailed him. He *couldn't* have been violent if she still had some desire to be in touch with him. If she still *loves* him, he must not have hurt her.

Their estimation of her—an estimation that is wildly ignorant when it comes to the mind-numbingly complex intricacies of domestic violence—will put her life in danger. The only chance she has is a one-page statement. She will have to read this statement in court in front of her ex-husband, a man who tried to kill her. She will have to read it in front of his slimy defense lawyer who is trying to paint her as a lying and vindictive alcoholic who has a deeply inconsistent narrative.

Hold on.

Did you just stop for a moment and wonder if maybe she *is* a lying and vindictive alcoholic? Or maybe not lying and vindictive, but an alcoholic, whose narrative might be inconsistent?

I did.

And I know how to identify this bias in my head before it does any damage. I can see that it runs counter to everything I know about Erica and women in abusive relationships. But it's still there anyway. Biases like these get planted by the media, bad science, and societal narratives long before we have any experience with the reality of the thing. We have been primed to be suspicious of the victim and empathetic to the perpetrator in cases like these, partly because going back to someone who has been violent to you does not seem rational. And we do not like to think that rational humans are capable of irrational behaviors, much less repetitive irrational behaviors.

I am drafting Erica's statement for her so that she doesn't have to stare at a blank page and try to write while fighting off the shame snake that slithers around her shoulders, already constricting her neck and stealing her breath. I am also drafting it because even though she may change everything about the statement, I want her to see in written form what I have already told her: that even though her behavior is inexplicable to herself, it is not inexplicable to me. This traumatic experience *can* be understood and processed and reconciled. I know because I've done it myself—more than once.

So here we are, begging for the kind of mercy no one should have to beg for.

How is it possible for Erica to still love this violent man? Why does she find herself reminiscing on their wedding anniversary? What on earth brought her to write an email to someone who she has worked so hard to get a restraining order against? What compels her to go against her rationality and go back to him time and again? How do we know that she won't go back again?

Sometimes we can only understand a complex thing through a simple metaphor.

Do you know about rare earth magnets? They are the strongest type of permanent magnets that exist. The energy between them, which forces them together, is so strong they can bruise skin and even break bones if a body part gets pinched between them. If two get too close to one another, they careen toward each other and can collide with such force that they shatter into shards.

Erica and her ex-husband are like rare earth magnets. Their relationship has the kind of magnetic energy that sends them careening toward each other. When they collide, her sense of self shatters into shards, making her and the universe inexplicable.

When this kind of rare earth magnetic force takes hold in a relationship, it is called a *trauma bond*. A trauma bond is an alchemical mix of unprocessed past experiences, uneven power dynamics, and contradictory behaviors that swing from violence to affection and back.

Trauma bonds are relational rare earth magnets—*dangerously attractive*.

TRAUMA BONDS

Let's get something out of the way right now: If you have experienced this kind of bond, you have not *manifested* it. You do not *attract* toxic people. You did not *ask* the universe for this kind of pain and confusion. Putting it this way is the psychological equivalent of saying that you are karmically responsible for your cancer diagnosis, or that God sends hurricanes to earth to smite us because some of us humans have the audacity to be homosexual. It's utter horseshit.

It actually would be easier if that horseshit was right. Then all we would have to do is simply decide to stop attracting toxic people. Unfortunately, trauma bonds are a good deal more complicated than that.

The term *trauma bond* is colloquially—and incorrectly—used to describe many different relationship dynamics. For example, you might hear of the intense bond that two soldiers develop because of what they survived together; they are said to be bonded by trauma. Or you might hear of the strange and fascinating psychological phenomenon whereby people who were abducted develop an affinity to their abductor; they are bonding in trauma. More recently, the term has come to represent a kind of relationship pattern among Instagram influencers who continue to find themselves in relationships with unsuitable folks; they are bonding with trauma.

The actual term comes from an especially tender spot in the history of trauma psychology: the study of violence in intimate relationships.

Here's a humbling piece of history: it was once the prevailing scientific belief that intimate violence was a result of a personality construct in the abused person. Let me be clear: it was thought that abuse was the fault of the person being abused. This was not just an idea floating around in society among the ignorant or uneducated, it was the *prevailing scientific theory*.

In the mid-1960s, researchers set out to understand physically abusive marriages. How did this happen and why? They first reached out to husbands who had been violent with their wives. Reluctant to talk or admit fault, the men unanimously aimed blame at their wives.

"It was her fault," they universally claimed, like a Greek chorus, shirking any responsibility. "I am a peaceful man, and I have never been violent before. She always knows just how to push my buttons, and she also knows that she will get a lot of sympathy afterward. She does it on purpose."

So the researchers reached out to the wives. Unlike their husbands, the women were not open or especially talkative. When asked about their own abusive marriages, they bristled. They were, on the whole, pretty detached, a little distant, and cold. They were completely indecisive and passive. Strangely, they all shared these traits, which made the researchers surmise that the husbands were right. Why else would all the women who had been abused have the same personality traits? The researchers concluded that there was a female personality type that brought up violence in otherwise peaceful men. These women, they speculated, *wanted* to be abused—*needed* to be abused. This personality type was a magnet that sent men's arms flailing. They were masochists.

Here's what is perhaps most striking about this entirely false correlation: *no one* paused to consider that perhaps it was the physical abuse that caused the personality traits in the women and not the other way around.

In the early 1980s, after twenty years of clinical treatment informed by the belief that if women are beaten by their husbands, it was because they wanted to be, researchers noticed that therapeutic methods based on this belief were ineffective. As it turns out, treating victims of violence with shame was not terribly effective. (*Shocker!*)

Two researchers in particular, Donald Dutton and Susan Painter, speculated that there was something about the *abuse* that changed the personality of the women. These women did not go back to violent relationships because they *wanted* to be abused; they went back because they had *lost their sense of self*. The bond between partners in these kinds of relationships seemed entirely unique. Dutton and Painter termed it a *traumatic bond*, which they defined as "the development and course of strong emotional ties between persons where one person intermittently harasses, beats, threatens, abuses or intimidates the other."[1]

Take note of the structures at work here: The magnetic force that sets this kind of terrible relationship into motion *does not lie in either of the members alone*. It is in the dynamic, and it is amplified—exponentially—by time, power, and shame.

As they studied these relationships, Dutton and Painter noticed two components that appeared again and again: an uneven power dynamic that one partner takes advantage of and abuse that is intermittent (rather than constant) and mixed with intense affection. Together, these components create devastating personality shifts in both people. As personalities become shaped around the relationship, a dangerously strong bond is formed and becomes very difficult to disengage from.

An uneven power dynamic is formed when one person is subjugated or dominated by the other. This can happen in any number of ways. One partner may have more money than the other, or one might hold a prestigious job that gives them an elevated social status, for example.

While it is possible for power imbalances to exist in relationships without violence or abuse, this imbalance alone is enough kindling to start a fire. That fire can be quelled, or it can be stoked. One especially effective fuel for this kind of fire is the exaggeration and diminishment of self-worth. It is easy to see how the partner with more power might begin to feel an exaggerated sense of worth, while the partner with less power comes to feel diminished in their overall sense of worth.

As time goes on, these feelings of worth and worthlessness can start to show up in both partners' behavior. The partner with more power might begin to see the less-powerful partner in a disparaging light and may start to treat them accordingly. This shift in treatment might worry the partner with less power, feeding into the fear that they are not good enough, and they might start to see themselves as worthless or as "less than" across the board. The less worthy they feel, the more needy they become, which then feeds right into the disparaging narrative that the partner with more power holds.

Imagine that a couple, Sam and Lauren, move from a small town to Manhattan after college. They move because Lauren has a great new job there and Sam hopes to find one within a few months. Lauren is the only one with a paycheck, so she pays all the bills. She is also the first to make friends, so she is the center of their social life.

Sam is happy for Lauren, but as time goes on and she is so clearly flourishing, he starts to feel down. Why can't he find a job as easily? He spends a few miserable hours in the morning applying for jobs and then waits around for Lauren to come home. She starts to feel irritated with him because when she gets home from a hard day at work, she is met with his low energy and neediness. She starts thinking maybe his pathetic affect is making it impossible for employers to see him as a go-getter. She starts criticizing him with an edge of frustration in her voice, hoping that he'll snap out of it and go back to his charming self. Instead, Sam starts feeling even lower.

When Lauren walks to work, she struggles to shake off Sam's mood. She deserves better than this—she *is* better than this. She makes all the money. Sam can't even get a job. All he does is complain about how hard everything is. What did she see in him to begin with? And he's starting to get chubby on top of it all. She comes home angry and resentful. The angrier she gets, the needier Sam gets. "He's so *pathetic*," she thinks. One night, she drinks too much and screams at Sam, kicking the criticism up several notches. She tells him that he'll never amount to anything, that he's fat and ugly, and that she deserves better. She smashes a wine glass against the kitchen sink and storms off into the night.

While this power dynamic is slowly eroding Sam's sense of self and making him come to believe he actually is worthless, the abusive behavior escalates. A set of criticisms meant to motivate become intense verbal abuse. A wine glass smashed in the sink out of frustration becomes a bottle thrown across the room, narrowly missing his head. Though it gets more intense, it is still mixed with authentically loving gestures and calm moments. Each time something dramatic happens, there is a wash of apologies, make-up sex, and promises that things will change. The back-and-forth is profoundly confusing and exhausting.

A lot of us think that we would never find ourselves in such a situation because as soon as we noticed the abuse, we would leave. A lot of us are wrong. We are wrong for two reasons.

The first is because we do not understand the chemical reactions that occur in this kind of dynamic. When we are tiny infants and have no ability to regulate our own physiology, we cry out for help whenever we feel distress. When we are soothed *after* feeling that distress, our brain is flooded with natural opioids. We then associate this connection—between distress and soothing—with pleasure. The brain develops this way to set up the neural priming it needs to associate relating to other people with reward. These chemicals help us become social and stay social, making survival more likely. They also help us develop techniques for co-regulating (soothing each other) and self-regulating (soothing ourselves).

This same physiological reaction can play out when, as adults, we experience conflict with another person, become distressed, and then are soothed—either by the other person in the conflict or by someone else. When we are soothed after our conflict-caused distress, we get a burst of happy chemicals. We can become addicted to these bursts—*not to conflict itself*, but to the feeling that comes from being soothed immediately after conflict.

The takeaway is this: on a neurobiological level, the cycle of abuse—*not the abuse itself*—can become addictive because there is a heavy dose of naturally occurring hormonal opioids during the upswing. This is *not* to say the abused person *wants* the abuse. In fact, quite the opposite. When someone in an abusive relationship is dysregulated and has had their power and sense of self stripped from them, they *need* the flood of soothing hormones. When these feel-good bursts do not come from outside of the relationship (partly because we are all *so fucking terrible* at supporting people in these relationships), the only option is to seek them out *within* the relationship.

The second reason we are wrong to assume this kind of thing could never happen to us is that there is no easier space to reconcile or forgive abusive behavior than within an intimate relationship.

Since the abusive behavior is balanced with times of intense connection, happiness, and intimacy, the abuse can seem like an accident, an aberration, a mistake that won't happen again and should really be kept secret so that other people don't get the wrong idea. "Lauren is stressed. She does have a really important job after all. Plus, someone who loves me this much surely couldn't have meant to hurt me like that," goes Sam's justification. Lauren even makes a joke of the abuse after an especially bad fight: "Our love is so passionate and intense that sometimes it gets a little out of control!" The conflict and abuse are portrayed as proof of deep love, not a refutation of it.

It is worth noting that the kind of power involved in these relationships is not one that belongs to one member or the other exclusively. Power is a force, and its charge can oscillate. There are moments where the abused partner comes to be *more* powerful than the abusive one, if only temporarily. This happens when the abused partner decides to leave, and the abuser flips into the subordinate role, begging for the abused partner to stay, lamenting their own terrible behavior, and promising things will be different this time. Though it looks like the previously powerless partner now has the power, the uneven power dynamic again works *against* the resolution of the abuse cycle.

The relationship bond can be especially strong because the longer the two people are in it, the more inscrutable they become to themselves. This is usually true of both people, as the individual identity of each person is given over to the dynamic between them. There is an underlying belief that the only way they can make sense of themselves and their behavior is by staying in the relationship.

One of the other reasons it is so harmful to reduce the complexity of a trauma bond to the idea that "I am attracting toxic people" is that there *is no such thing as toxic people*. Lauren is not a toxic *person*—she is *behaving* in a toxic way. Her behavior is due to a set of circumstances and dynamics that may have made her inexplicable to herself.

This is not to excuse her from responsibility or to say her behavior is acceptable. Abuse is *never* acceptable. It is to say that if we want to stop cycles of abuse, we need to *understand* them. And to understand them, we need to move beyond the idea that Lauren is toxic or that Sam is attracting toxicity. Because when we reduce complicated relationship dynamics in this way, we miss the point.

Lauren does not wake up the morning after throwing a bottle at Sam and take him out to brunch because she is evil and manipulative. She does it as an attempt to repair behavior that she does not understand herself. In a trauma bond, *both* people are caught in the magnetic force. *Both* are destabilized. *Both* are at risk of shattering the more they collide.

REPEATING THE TRAUMA BOND

Remember Erica, the woman I was ventriloquizing in the court letter? I am about to tell you something about Erica that might make you doubt her even more than when you spent a minute or two wondering if she was an alcoholic.

This is not her first abusive relationship. We can't even say that it will be her last.

What we know so far are the components of a trauma bond. We know that this kind of bond contains an alchemical mix of power dynamics and a confusing back-and-forth of positive and negative treatment. We know the bond gradually rips away the abused partner's sense of self and makes it nearly impossible for them to leave. And we know that because their sense of self has been so destabilized, they often return as soon as they feel anxiety or insecurity out in the world.

We can begin to understand how someone may find themselves in an isolated trauma bond, but what about someone who continues to get entangled in trauma bonds in different relationships throughout their life? Is this a case of someone manifesting or attracting abuse?

No. Still no.

Let me fast-forward a little bit and tell you how Erica's story unfolds. Against all odds, the statement we coauthored for the court works. The begged-for mercy comes. The judge is persuaded by her statement, believes her, grants her the restraining order, and even gives her ex-husband double jail time. For a few days, Erica feels free.

And then she is overcome with guilt for putting him in jail. And then she misses him. And then she notices she still fantasizes about him, is still attracted to him. So when he reaches out because he needs some bills paid, she helps him. And when he starts telling her he's really going to use this time to change, she believes him a little bit—again.

I tell her what her therapist has already told her, what her friends have told her, what her family has told her, and what she has read.

"Erica, next time, he's *going* to kill you."

"I know," she says. "I don't understand myself."

Her face doesn't fall when she says this, but only because it was already fallen. She doesn't understand herself.

We are still missing pieces.

THE REPETITION COMPULSION

One of the missing pieces points back to Freud, so back to the 1900s we go.

In 1914, Freud wrote an article called, "Remembering, Repeating, and Working-Through." In it, he noted how strange it was that rather than remembering a negative experience or relationship dynamic and avoiding it, the patient would simply repeat it. And repeat it. And repeat it. *Ad nauseum.* This kind of thing is important because if we misunderstand the sources of our behavior, *all* our relationships become really confusing. We also run the risk of living our entire lives in repetition of the most negative experiences and dynamics that we encounter.

In 1920, Freud further explored this idea in his famous work "Beyond the Pleasure Principle," which might as well have been called, "Why Our Behavior Is Sometimes Completely and Fascinatingly

Inexplicable." In the essay, he classified four kinds of repetitive behavior that seem to run counter to what he thought was the innate and primary human drive toward pleasure.

The first kind of repetition Freud wrote about was the way an event would appear and reappear in dreams. These could be recurring dreams directly replaying the event, or dreams with wandering content that repeated the core emotions of the event. In either case, the dreams seemed to put the patient "back into the [terrible] situation" rather than "showing the patient pictures from his healthy past."[2] Though our lives are populated with all sorts of wonderful and pleasure-filled experiences, we don't tend to have intrusive dreams about *those*. Why would our mind reflect the bad stuff back to us so much more often?

The second kind of repetition showed up in children's play. Freud described watching a child throw his toy from his crib, cry at his loss, and then work to reel the toy back in—all to just throw the toy again and repeat the distressing cycle. I remember sharing a bedroom on a family vacation with my little brother who did this for what felt like an entire week straight. I was probably six, and remember vividly trying to understand *why* he would toss his pacifier across the room as soon as someone got out of bed to hand it back to him.

The third kind of repetition is when a patient attempted to explain a traumatic event from the past and slipped into reliving it in the midst of retelling it. Freud noted that patients seemed to be repeating traumatic experiences as if they were "contemporary experiences instead of, as the physician would prefer to see, *remembering* it as something belonging to the past."[3] Traumatic memories seemed to collapse the walls between past and present, rendering the world an unnavigable contradiction.

The fourth and most haunting kind of repetition was termed *Schicksalzwang*, or fate neurosis. This is when traumatic experiences escape the boundaries of the mind and play out in behavioral repetition. Patients would find themselves repeating unpleasant relationship dynamics and life experiences without being aware that they were doing it and without being able to stop. This kind of repetition vexed Freud the most. Wasn't living through the terrible event *once* bad enough? To what possible end would patients repeatedly put themselves into situations in which they had to relive their most terrible life experiences again and again?

These repetitive tendencies challenged Freud's theory that human behavior is fundamentally aimed toward experiencing pleasure. If human beings are pleasure-seeking creatures, why in the hell did they so consistently repeat their most terrible and painful experiences?

Sensing the compulsive force at the heart of these seemingly inexplicable behaviors, Freud concluded that the drive to repeat negative experiences came from something "more primitive, more elementary, more instinctual than the pleasure principle which it over-rides."[4] This impulse to repeat came from somewhere else, somewhere much darker than most human impulses. He concluded that this kind of compulsion to repeat gave the impression of "a daemonic" compulsion.[5] This seems worth pausing to emphasize: this destructive impulse to repeat was so powerful and so dark that the only way Freud could understand it was to define it as an otherworldly and *demonic* force.

A compulsion is a force that cannot be resisted—a driving, *urgent* force. The word *compulsion* comes from the Latin *com*, meaning "with, together," and *pellere*, meaning "to drive; to thrust, strike." If we are to use the language of manifestation or the law attraction here, we *cannot* mean it in a sense that involves willing or choosing. The force that drives us to repeat the cycle is not one we choose. It is an impulse that comes from the core of our experience and drives us forward in ways that look baffling only later.

The compulsion to repeat is well documented and even appears in cases in which people have no access to a conscious memory of what they are repeating. Often the repetition happens on the exact anniversary of the initial event—again, *even though people do not have a conscious memory of that initial event*. There are cases where people repeat an event on that same day for years in a row even though it causes them great pain and sometimes puts them in very real danger.

This is an especially cruel truth about traumatic experience: it cannot be hemmed in by time, it does not obey the normal rules of temporal form, and it does not restrict itself to the moment in which it occurs. We are haunted by traumatic events in one way or another—in our thoughts, in our dreams, and sometimes in the actions we are driven to repeat.

Does this cruel truth contain within it anything other than cruelty? Why must we be haunted? Why must we relive? What *is* this force that compels us? And what is its purpose? What can be done about these ghosts?

REASONS TO REPEAT

I once attended a lecture given by Galen Strawson, an angry academic who was trying to argue against all of science and philosophy that the self is not narrative. Sir Christopher Ricks, a literary critic and scholar, gave a graceful, scathing, and deeply satisfying response: "The trouble seems to be, dear Strawson, that you seem entirely taken up by the wrong question. The important question is *never* 'is this true?' It is '*what truth is there in this?*'"[6]

Since Freud brought attention to the repetition compulsion in the late 1800s, the field of psychology has been arguing *which* explanation of the behavior is correct. Framing the discussion this way is to be taken up by the wrong question. There is not a singular reason that explains or captures this "demonic force" that compels us to relive. The truth is there are many reasons we find ourselves replicating behaviors and relationship dynamics. Let's look at a few of those while tacitly acknowledging that what follows can only ever be a partial list.

We Repeat in Order to Master

Freud's initial theory was that we repeat our negative experiences in the hopes that we might master them. From a theoretical perspective, this makes sense. When we are so overwhelmed by an experience that we flee, fight, or freeze, this experience is bound to stick out and defy integration because it does not get processed and filed away like our other memories. We then are driven to reexperience it because doing so gives us the chance to master an experience that, in real life, defied mastery.

We relive so that we can have the opportunity to understand what we could not comprehend in the initial overwhelming moment, and so that we might get a chance to respond differently than we did during the initial event.

Though Freud could not have known it, this theory bears out in neurobiology too. Unintegrated memories are a problem for the brain. As an attempt to integrate them, the brain will push them forward in some way—in dreams, intrusive thoughts, and repetitive situations—so that they get sorted and put away properly.

You'll remember from chapter 2 that our brains are designed with a sophisticated filing system that helps us order and archive our memories so that we can learn from the world and understand our experience. The neurobiological term for the filing process is *memory consolidation*. The way memories get initially consolidated depends on the type of experience and how we perceive the event when it is happening. Run-of-the-mill, normal experiences do not cause overwhelm in the brain, and so when they are organized and put away, all necessary filing systems are up and running. When all systems are online and working as they are supposed to, the events we experience go through a consolidation (and then reconsolidation) process. You will remember that long-term memories are filed away primarily in the hippocampus, and each file needs to contain three things: a coherent narrative of the event, emotional content from the event, and a meaning that we have settled on in order to contextualize the event according to our other memories. As a result, these memory files end up pretty organized and accessible. We can pull these memories into present consciousness, talk about them, and then put them away with relative ease.

Initial memory consolidation—the part when the file is created and its contents are organized—typically happens between six and twenty-four hours after an event. You can think of little workers in a file room in your brain. All they do is sort through what you experience and figure out how to archive it correctly. What does it mean? Where does it fit in among the other files? These little workers are fastidious and hardworking. They store things according to chronology and meaning so that you can recall what you need quickly.

When it comes to traumatic experience—when you have an overwhelming emotional experience—the workers in the recording and the filing room give all of their energy and resources to the alarm system and protective mechanisms in your brain. Filing does not need to be done when you are actively in danger; that can be sorted out later. So instead of having a consolidated and organized memory file, the file is created but is disorganized in one of many possible ways. These memories are a bit like corrupted computer files. They either can't be opened at all, or, when they do open, they do so at random and interrupt what you were trying to do. What we find inside the files is difficult to make sense of. We don't speak its code.

Luckily, or perhaps unluckily, depending on how you look at it, our brain has a method for dealing with disorganized files. Whenever the little workers in the file room come face-to-face with one of these files, they simply toss it into the prefrontal cortex (which is where most memory consolidation occurs) to be processed again. This is lucky because it gives us the opportunity to organize and put away the event in a way that we couldn't before. It is unlucky because when a disorganized traumatic memory gets tossed into the prefrontal cortex, we do not recognize it as a past memory because it isn't organized like all of our other memories. The only possible way to relate to it is to relive it.

So while memories are consolidated in the first six to twenty-four hours after an experience, they are also *reconsolidated* over and over again afterward. This reconsolidation can be done consciously and on purpose—this is what we are doing in narrative therapy, for example—but it is also being done in the brain unconsciously. The little file organizers don't just work with current events. They also continually comb through old files to make sure they don't need updating given new information and experience. Like any other file room, our memory has limited space, and so sometimes the workers have to get rid of old memories in order to make room for new ones. Think of this process as what your laptop does when you empty the trash and hit "restart."

We live out this reconsolidation process when we have experiences that challenge our understanding of someone. Think, for example, of the thought processes that happen when you are betrayed by a partner. If you find out that your spouse has been having an affair, you will find yourself consciously and unconsciously combing through memory files from your relationship and updating information in them. This happens when you sit down to journal about the betrayal and try to find red flags that you missed. And it also happens when you are on a hike and trying to enjoy your day, and memories get pushed forward that you haven't thought about in years.

This mechanism is what makes it possible to reassign meaning to events from the past, to change how we think and feel about them, and to relate to them differently when we consider our larger identity. It is also the source of some of the most painful symptoms of traumatic experience: intrusive thoughts, rumination, nightmares, and panic attacks.

This mechanism is also part of what is at work in repetition compulsion. The quickest way to reconsolidate a memory is to have an identical one to place right next to it for comparison. When we do not have the necessary components to rework a memory file—when we are missing pieces of the narrative or missing the narrative altogether, for example— putting ourselves right back into the same situation is an efficient way to gather the missing components.

We Repeat to Avoid Mastery

Bessel van der Kolk, a psychiatrist and trauma researcher, disagrees with Freud on the idea that we repeat in order to master. Van der Kolk argues this cannot be correct because the repetition "leads only to further pain and self-hatred."[7] On one hand, he is right: repetition does lead to further pain and self-hatred. On the other hand, just because pain and self-hatred are the results doesn't mean that repetition is aimed at producing them. Repeating a traumatic experience or relationship dynamic is a coping technique. All our coping is aimed at regulation, and some of it over time becomes maladaptive and destructive. Whether the result is healthy and productive or unhealthy and destructive, the goal of any coping mechanism is always integration and regulation.

We also must consider that sometimes the stakes involved in integrating an experience are much higher than remaining dysregulated and locked in repeating patterns. Sometimes it's much easier to *repeat* a dynamic than it is to admit what is *behind* that dynamic.

Remember, our memory files don't simply have narrative and emotional content, they also have *meaning*. If we have foundational life experiences that are abusive, it can mean one of only three things to our brain: there is something wrong with us, the world is terrible and all people are abusive, or the abusers simply did not love us. All these possibilities are tragic and heartbreaking, but the third is perhaps the worst—especially if the abusers were our parents.

Sometimes opening ourselves up to further abuse is a way to protect our original abusers—not simply because we want to absolve them, but because of what it would mean if we didn't.

We Repeat Because It Feels like Home

I am sitting at a boardroom table and the CEO of the small nonprofit I work for is screaming and sweating and turning red. He's over six feet tall, and he's towering above me and my colleagues, as if his stature and booming, aggressive voice didn't establish the power dynamic clearly enough. I have no idea what he's yelling about. I lost the thread long ago. The sun is streaming through the French doors of the conference room and onto the table, turning it so blindingly white that it makes everything in my peripheral vision pink. I can feel a headache coming on. I'm floating somewhere behind perception, completely checked out.

Suddenly, the six-foot-tall, red, screaming man folds in half and sits down dramatically, as if he has been taken out by a sniper's bullet. A switch somewhere deep inside of him flips and he is a different version of himself altogether. Instead of yelling and spitting, he's now breathing slower and speaking in dulcet tones, reminding us that, "above all, the order is God, family, and *then* work." He splays his hands out as if he is a holy figure saying grace at a beautiful meal, as if the screaming that just happened was part of a spiritual ritual—a necessary kind of purge before the great awakening.

As soon as this switch flips, something inside of me flips too. I come plunging back into my body, and my heart rate shoots up into the 180s even though I'm sitting still. There is a sudden metallic taste of adrenaline at the back of my throat, and I can feel my skin flush a burning dark red. I go from not being present in my body at all to wanting to smash everything in the room just to get out. I ignore everything happening in my body as best I can. Chalk it up to general anxiety.

And then he takes us all out to dinner. We walk down the boardwalk toward the restaurant, thick as thieves, laughing conspiratorially, as if we have just left a completely normal work meeting, as if nothing has happened at all.

Later that night, I'm relaying the story to a friend when I get the first signal that maybe my brain has attached the wrong meaning to the memory file. I'm telling the story as if it's a "listen to this silly thing my boss did today" kind of story.

"Yelling is never okay," my friend says, as if it were obvious.

"Well, it's a start-up, it's stressful, and we've got this board meeting . . . ," I start to justify.

"Yelling is never okay," he repeats.

"I mean, everyone gets to that point . . ."

"Sure. Still. Yelling is never okay."

He didn't know it, but that sentence, repeated gently three times, brought tears to my eyes, and I had to lie down to stop them.

I thought about this four-word sentence for months: yelling is never okay.

Part of me *really* wanted to resist this idea. In my life, there had *always* been yelling. This dynamic started at home, with my mom. Whenever she started to feel out of control or afraid, there was yelling. And yelling. And yelling. And then, just like that, the switch would flip, and there was a wash of kindness and normalcy—never an apology, but a righting of the world that had just been turned upside down.

Part of me knows that there never should have been yelling. That you shouldn't learn when you are *very* small that the best way to handle a situation is to figure out how to spin backward out of your body and away from reality until you can't quite hear or see. That someone should have stopped it. But they didn't, and so my trauma response was shaped by this. And it's been a dynamic that I've repeated.

I'd like to say that there have only been two situations like this in my life, but that would be a lie. There have been many—*many*, many. They didn't register. I couldn't understand them. I couldn't regard them as unacceptable because they felt familiar. I chalked my body response up to anxiety. I assumed I was broken. For example, I didn't leave that job when I should have because that out-of-control and abusive behavior was normal to me. I didn't see it that way because it felt like home.

I was in that job, by the way, to teach them about the trauma response, the symptoms of which are so brilliant and adaptive that even the experts miss them.

We Repeat Because of Our Neurobiology: The Mohawk of Self-Awareness

In a perfectly accidental combination of punk-rock aesthetic and brain structure, it turns out that all the parts of our brain associated with knowing ourselves run down the center of the brain, from just above our eyes to the back of the head—you know, like a pink mohawk.

You can think of this pink mohawk as the most self-assured, rebellious, decisive, little badass version of yourself. She knows where she is (the posterior cingulate gives us a sense of where we are in space), what kinds of music and art she loves passionately (the parietal lobes are responsible for integrating sensory information), what she feels (the insula brings messages from perception to the emotion centers), what she thinks about how she feels (the anterior cingulate coordinates emotions and thinking), and what she is going to do about it (the medial prefrontal cortex is critical in decision-making processes).

Researchers have found that in untraumatized folks, the mohawk of self-awareness is lit up frequently. In a healthy brain there is a near constant process of checking in with yourself and using inner and outer experiences to strengthen your sense of self. Bodily experience, thought, and emotions are all integrated, and energy flows between these areas of the brain to unite and understand them.

In traumatized folks, on the other hand, there is *sharply* decreased activity in the mohawk of self-awareness. In people with chronic PTSD, there is almost none. It is dim, dull. This means that the parts of the brain responsible for integrating sensory information, noticing fluctuations in bodily experience, communicating emotional experience, and making decisions are essentially offline. And when they are, it is much harder to be aware and connected with internal states and much harder to make sense of the external world, let alone make any forward motion within it.

Remember the women from the battered wives study in the 1960s? They all shared the same personality traits of being cold, disconnected, passive, and unable to make decisions. They all appeared that way because their traumatic experience had altered their brain function.

Hold on, though. If the trauma response is adaptive, how can this altering of brain function make sense? Why would the brain disconnect from the parts that could help us recognize and remove ourselves from abusive situations?

Because sometimes the quickest and most effective adaptation is to *stop feeling altogether.*

In response to overwhelming traumatic experiences, the brain learns to shut down the parts of it that register and detail those horrible experiences. If you can't escape a terrible situation, the best way to survive is to feel *less*, notice *less*, think *less*. It's both a brilliant and heartbreaking response. It can save someone from crushing overwhelm in the moment, but over a long period of time, it can lead to an inability to see oneself *as* a self, to make decisions as an individual, and to read the emotions of others—all of which can lead to further victimization.

In other words: we repeat dangerous or damaging experiences because we have lost ourselves neurobiologically.

Again, these are only four possible things that can compel us to repeat our most terrible life experiences. There are likely many, many more. Perhaps detailing all of them is not as important as knowing how to reconnect to ourselves when we're in a cycle of repetition.

THE SHARDS

After I'm done with the draft of Erica's statement, I send an email to my dear friend Chris. I don't tell him anything about Erica, of course, or the statement we're writing together. I just rant and rave for a couple of paragraphs about rare earth magnets. I explain how they can break bones if the body is pinched between them. And that if two of them are allowed to get too close to one another, they can strike with such force that the material shatters. I also share that the flying shards can cause injury.

When I wake up in the morning, there's an email from Chris waiting for me. He tells me a story about visiting an art festival with his wife:

> There is one particular case of jewelry that catches my eye. Inside are tiny silver disks, about half the diameter of a dime, that are linked together to make bracelets. I ask the designer about the designs on the disks, which look like they might be Chinese characters but are clearly not Chinese characters. "Are these random, or are they intentional?"
>
> "Completely random."
>
> Then she tells us that she had silver shavings left over from the other pieces. "The main pieces," she might have said. She didn't want to go through the hassle of sending the shavings back to her supplier to be melted down, so now, when she has enough shards, she lets them fall randomly together on these disks, applies just enough heat to let them hold together, but not so much that they melt completely together. Not so much that they lose their individual shapes. No. You can still see the unique silver strands, some the diameter of corn silk, that have come together and reflect light differently and in the most beautiful, and now we know, completely random way.
>
> And not to hit you over the head with it, but I'm struck that these pieces, the most lovely in the whole art show, are the remnants. The shards.

This is the last missing piece: the shards. We're misunderstanding the shards left by our traumatic experience and what those shards do to the trauma response. We're getting them wrong because we soak our traumatic experiences and our response to them in shame. We marinate in that shame until shame is all that we can see, all that we are, all that runs through our veins.

It's not the way we responded to the initial trauma that is the problem, it is our *shame about* the way we responded. Our shame about the strange magnetism that lies underneath some of our behavior. Our shame at knowing our behavior sent shards scattering each time we collided with the person our trauma bond keeps us connected to. Our shame about how we kept repeating our behavior, our terrible experiences, anyway.

The shards can be dangerous, and they might cause injury. But they can also catch the light and *shine*. They can be the loveliest pieces.

This may seem counter to everything I've written here. It may even seem disrespectful.

When Erica looks at her story, all she sees is pain and suffering and inexplicable behavior. When researchers looked at domestic abuse in the 1960s, they came up with a pathology that some people need pain. When Freud looked at the repetition compulsion, he saw a demonic force at work that could not be understood.

The incredible force inside the rare earth magnet pulls it toward *unity*. The incredible internal force that sends us careening toward someone who causes us pain is always aimed at *adaptation*. The shards are proof— not of our brokenness, but of that tremendous adaptive force. That is why they shine. That is why they are lovely.

Once we know about this force, once we are aware of its tremendous strength, once we can look at it in the light instead of soaking it in shame, we can *direct* it.

TAKEAWAYS AND TOOLS

There isn't a tool that will single-handedly extract you from a harmful relationship. There isn't a tool that will swiftly sever the chains of a trauma bond. There isn't a tool that will make sure you avoid all harmful relationships in the future. There isn't *a* tool. For this, you need *all* the tools. You need a therapist. You need a strong support network. You need the painful awareness that even when you use all the tools you may still find yourself humbled and bruised, sitting dazed in the wreckage that a collision between rare earth magnets has caused, yet again.

And.

There are tools for hope, tools that remind you that even amidst all the wreckage, hope is still there—gritty and glinting, resilient and stead-fast. This is not sunshine-and-rainbow hope. This is the kind of hope that drags itself back to its feet after being sucker punched, spits out a mouthful of blood, maybe a tooth, and keeps going despite its ringing ears and wobbly knees. This is the kind of hope that stands right next to you while you peer into the dark and roiling abyss, takes a deep breath, and says, "Okay. Now what?"

LEARNED HELPLESSNESS, LEARNING HOPE

One of the reasons battered woman syndrome prevailed for so long is the way it corresponded with the behavioral theory about the effects of traumatic experience on someone's personality. Before we knew about the brain mechanisms involved in responding to traumatic events, it was thought that after aversive events helplessness became a learned trait. In other words, helplessness was a fixed and global stance rather than an emotion tied to an overwhelming event or set of tricky circumstances. The theory was that once you had been knocked down by a traumatic experience, your behavior became modified to operate from a place of hopelessness. This change made it very difficult to escape bad situations because you now believed it was impossible to experience anything other than bad things. If that was true, what would you be escaping into, exactly? A different kind of bad? No thanks. Why bother?

This theory—that we learn helplessness and it then becomes a personality trait—came from research done by Martin Seligman and Steven Maier in the late 1960s. Seligman and Maier speculated that when animals were repeatedly exposed to aversive events, they learned that their actions did not impact these events; the animals learned that they were fundamentally helpless in the world. This lesson, in turn, made it impossible for the animals to escape future aversive situations, even when the escape route seemed simple and obvious. They were operating under a global belief that nothing they did mattered. In other words, they had learned helplessness.

This idea that aversive events can lead to a global helpless feeling and general passivity became the prevailing theory to explain why people sometimes stay in and repeatedly get into abusive relationships.

Fifty years later, Seligman and Maier realized they had the theory backward. It was indeed true that when repeatedly exposed to aversive events, people tend to shut down and become helpless, but *not* because they learn this behavior. Instead, it is because the trauma response kicks into overdrive. When a situation is bad and goes on for long enough, the trauma response—which, again, is part of our default wiring designed for *strength and survival*—shuts us down. The act of shutting down in a bad situation preserves energy and makes it more likely that we will survive. If exposed to enough negative and dangerous circumstances, the system shuts down and *stays* shut down.

What that means is that depression and passivity in response to aversive events is not a learned behavior. It is the default evolutionary response. In other words, what was happening in the aftermath of traumatic experience was neurobiological, *not* behavioral.

Let me put that even more directly: when you are in a bad situation, sometimes you get stuck where you are because in what is designed to be a protective mechanism, your neurobiology has made it impossible to leave.

This fact may seem quite damning. It might seem like we are wired to work against ourselves, to stay *stuck* despite the rational awareness that we need some traction. It's not. We just need to stare into the abyss just a tiny bit longer.

"Okay," says that gritty and glinting hope, "now what?"

The best way to understand what happens and find hope is to think about brain circuitry just like electrical circuitry in a house. The latter is sometimes baffling, especially if you don't have insight into what's behind the walls. When you move into a new house, you quickly learn how much electrical activity the house can handle. You might find that if you run the air conditioner at the same time as your hair dryer, a fuse blows. Or you discover that the microwave and the dishwasher can't both be turned on without all the lights in the living room flickering. The general idea is that the electrical circuits can only handle so much, and that everything can't be running all at the same time.

Your brain circuitry is the same. Since the brain alters blood flow and electrical activity in response to internal and external stimuli, it is often shifting energy from one circuit to another. Certain circuits in the brain cannot be on at the same time as others because they require too much energy—just like the air conditioner and the hair dryer.

The precise way that brain circuitry works is not necessary to understand. All we need is a general idea of which switches control which circuits and which circuits take too much energy from the others.

The two circuits we are concerned about can be called the fear circuit and the hope circuit. When the fear circuit is turned on by aversive shock, it takes lots and *lots* of energy away from the other circuits. *This* is what prohibits escape. The parts of the brain needed to see escape as an option, plan it out, and execute the plan are offline when the fear circuit has been switched on. So escape becomes *neurobiologically impossible*. No matter how much you want to run the air conditioner and the hair dryer at the same time, you can't. So you adapt by toggling circuits on and off. You turn off the air conditioner and run the hair dryer, turn off the hair dryer and turn the air conditioner back on.

We can do the same workaround in our brains. Though the shutdown that comes from the fear circuit being switched on *feels* permanent and outside of our control, it is not. This fear circuit can be dampened if we toggle to another circuit that cannot be online at the same time: *the hope circuit*, as Seligman and Maier have termed it.

Just like the fear circuit, the hope circuit requires all sorts of energy and electrical activity. That means that when it is switched on, the fear center *has* to switch off. One way to alter electrical flow in our brain is through our thoughts. By thinking about the measurable and real control we have over our current situation, we can turn on the hope circuit. Leaning into the feeling of control counters the feeling of passivity.

Have doubts? I get it. It doesn't seem like it could be this simple to turn off something as powerful as our fear circuit. But let me show you.

I want you to imagine a lemon sitting on a cutting board on the kitchen counter. The lemon is a perfect yellow color. The light is streaming in from the window and falling diagonally across the cutting board. You pick up your best knife and cut the lemon in half. Immediately juice starts to bead on the surface of the freshly cut halves. Lemon drops roll and glisten in the sun, and as you take a deep breath, the smell of lemon is almost overwhelming—bright and strong and fresh. After your next deep breath, you pick up one of the lemon halves and take a big bite, really digging your teeth into the flesh of the fruit. Your mouth puckers as the tart juice fills it.

Just now, as you read that paragraph, did your mouth started watering? Even just a little? I bet that it did. See? You just used your thoughts to change your biology.

You didn't actually bite into a lemon. Your mouth started watering at the *thought* of biting into a lemon. You changed your neurobiological response with an *idea*. It wasn't even your idea; it was one you read. What does this prove? That what we think about changes our brain, and what changes our brain changes our biology.

When you are thinking about things you are afraid of, your thoughts switch on the fear circuit, and your body will start to feel activated. Instantly, you will notice this circuitry reverberate through your body. Your heart rate might go up. You might start sweating just a bit. You might feel a constriction in your stomach, a sudden sharpened sense of alertness, a straightening of your spine. You might notice these things happening even if you rationally know that you are not in danger. The same thing happens when you watch a scary movie with friends; you can feel fear in your body even though you rationally know that you are safe.

The circuitry works the other way as well. If you stop and focus on something that makes you laugh, someone you love, or your rambunctious pet, the fear lifts and dissipates like fog burning off in the afternoon sun. In its place you will feel calm and peace spread through your body like a gentle wave. You will feel a loosening where there was a gripping and a dampening or blurring in your senses where there was laser-sharp intensity.

Switching on the hope circuit with your thoughts will make you feel less fear, less helplessness, more hope, and more possibility. The fear circuit and the hope circuit operate like counterweights—lift one and the other automatically lowers.

How do you switch on the hope circuit? Here are two quick exercises.

TRAUMA TOOL: RECALIBRATE YOUR SPHERE OF INFLUENCE

Central to the experience of helplessness is the feeling that one has no sphere of influence whatsoever. When an individual is reeling from a traumatic experience or living through a current traumatic situation, their brain is stuck in the fear circuit, and the word *helpless* thrums through their body as frequently and regularly as their own heartbeat.

We may think that making big changes is the only way to prove that we have influence over our lives. This thinking is problematic in a couple of ways. To start, we are looking at situations in which big change feels *impossible*. Forcing ourselves to make big changes from that deep of a deficit sets us up for failure. Even if it works in the short term, it often fails in the long term because it frames our agency as black and white. We are either completely free or not free at all. At the first sign of an obstacle, we are proven wrong again, and we are back to believing that we are *fully* helpless—blind, mewling kittens in an existential basket.

What is more effective is to focus on the many, many places where we do have influence. When we feel really stuck and are convinced that there are no such places, it is incredibly powerful to find just how many tiny ones are littered around us.

Step 1: Right now, while you read, think about the various actions you could take in this moment. They can be tiny or more substantial. You get to decide.

Step 2: Choose one or two to complete.

Step 3: As you are completing your task(s), focus on how many possibilities there were and how it feels to choose one and complete it.

Coming up empty? Here are just a few examples.

You might get up and close the window, open the curtains, turn on a lamp, get an Advil or a cookie, or make a cup of tea. You might close this book (even though it's awesome) and come back later. You might lie on the floor and stretch your back. You might pick up your phone and play Tetris because all this talk of helplessness and abuse has made you feel a little overwhelmed. You might call your sister, or turn the light out and go to sleep. You might put your reading glasses on, or turn to your other side, fluff a pillow, pet your dog. You might get up and walk over to the thermostat and turn up the heat. You might go into the kitchen and load one dish into the dishwasher and leave the rest in the sink. You might change your laundry or go see if you have a lemon in the fridge. You might put your hiking shoes on and walk out the door, or decide to clean out your car. You might pick up your water glass and take three sips, counting each one. You might take three deep breaths and try to remember where your diaphragm is. You might go looking in your kitchen for pasta sauce, thinking about what to make for dinner. You might google what it's like to have a bunny as a pet or go searching for fancy houses on Zillow so you can make fun of the stuffy decor. You might light a scented candle or eat some potato chips or turn on reality TV.

Each time you think of a list of tiny actions you can take and then choose one or two of them to complete—no matter how small—you are restoring the sense of control and expectancy in your brain. Why does this work? Because the awareness of control is one of the switches in the hope circuit. By focusing on things that you can control, you are switching off the fear circuit. This inhibits the fear center and turns the lights out on the feeling of helplessness.

One last thing: A key part of what makes traumatic experience—and perhaps especially those that occur within abusive relationships—so shattering is that you lose access to yourself as a self. You stop seeing yourself as someone who has a unique personality, someone who can make decisions and follow through on them.

One of the brain structures that operates within the hope circuit matrix is the medial-prefrontal cortex. You will remember from earlier in the chapter that this structure is part of the mohawk of self-awareness and is critical to decision-making processes. By focusing on your sphere of influence and making tiny little decisions, you are not just shifting how you feel in the moment, but you are also reconnecting with the part of your brain that recognizes you as a self. Over time, restoring the neural connectivity to this part of your brain helps you become you again.

TRAUMA TOOL: ABSURD HOPE

At a particularly hard time in my life, I found myself plunged into complete and utter darkness—the kind that swallows everything and pushes you down into the ground. I could barely stand up in the morning and constantly felt as if gravity were trying to pull me into the fiery center of the earth. I didn't have the energy to shower before work or even put on real pants. I couldn't bear to sit at my desk. I dabbed on concealer and mascara so I might look like a human who slept, signed on to my computer in pajama pants and tossed a scarf around my neck to hide the fact that I was wearing a stretched-out T-shirt with holes in it. In between sessions I would lie on the floor next to my coffee table and listen to construction noises and crows while staring up at the ceiling. At the end of the day, I traded my pajama pants for yoga pants and dragged myself to the studio. During *Savasana* (Corpse Pose) I cried silently on my mat.

During this time, I happened to be researching the hope circuit. I came across an exercise that advocated for dreaming about your future life, and no matter how many times I tried to do it, all I felt were sparks of rage. Hope felt ridiculous and absurd, like a luxury I couldn't possibly afford. *What* future life? Everything seemed impossible when I was spending every ounce of energy I had trying to survive the moment, and the next, and the next.

My rage was offset by the fact that the brain science was so convincing.

I wanted to use hope to build a bridge between an impossible future and a possible one. It occurred to me that part of what makes the hope circuit light up was imagining the future in great detail. It didn't matter if the future actually *happened.* What mattered was that the brain was changing in that imagining stage.

So for five days, I set aside fifteen minutes a day to imagine a future in as much detail as possible. But I made sure it was a future I knew wasn't going to happen. I imagined myself as a ballerina living in Paris. I wore cashmere leg warmers and tulle tutus. I had a beret and a bicycle and a basket with a baguette in it. My apartment had a skylight in the kitchen, which squeaked terribly whenever I opened it. I sipped sparkling rosé in the evening and had a group of lovely friends.

The next day, I imagined I was the owner of a tiny flower shop in Savannah, Georgia. We had peonies year-round and were famous for it. I spent half the day preparing peonies for shipment to other states and countries and felt a little conflicted about it. If peonies were suddenly always available, would they be less special? I had a older golden retriever who came to work and snored behind the counter.

You get the point.

Within just five days, I noticed a marked change in myself. I had much more energy; I stopped lying on the floor in between sessions and instead got up and did things. I showered before work and sat at my desk. I still cried on the yoga mat at the end of the day, but it felt less labored and scary. Despite myself, I started to notice possibility again. The sunshine stopped feeling oppressive and started feeling like an invitation to come outside and take a walk. I know this seems like an exaggeration—that it shouldn't be possible to feel that much change that quickly—but believe me when I tell you that I was entirely skeptical too. The thing is, it *worked*.

Since then, I've tried it with groups and individual clients. I discovered that this tool didn't work for just me; it works in general.

Sometimes you can't make a big change or understand why you're in the situation you are in. But you can always flip your circuitry. And that will always make a difference, even though that difference might be tiny. Here's how you can do this exercise.

> **Step 1:** Block off fifteen minutes of your day for yourself. Silence your phone and turn off the TV. If it's hard for you to disconnect, do this exercise in the shower or on a walk or while your car goes through the car wash.

> **Step 2:** Dream up a ridiculous life for yourself—one that you *know* is impossible. Pick a setting from a movie plot. Imagine yourself as an astronaut even though you're an accountant, or as a billionaire Brazilian plastic surgeon even though you work in retail.

> **Step 3:** Enter that life like you're turning on a movie. Imagine the scene in as vivid detail as possible. What are you wearing? What does the place look like? What kinds of friends do you have? What do you do for fun?

> **Step 4:** Do this dreaming every single day for fifteen minutes and see what shifts in a week.

There are two reasons that I am suggesting that you think up a scenario that is absurd. First, it gives you more creative permission. You can imagine things that are totally absurd and impossible (being a dog, for example) rather than trying to spend time searching for something that is within reach and trying to bend to the limitations of reality. Second, if you're spending time thinking about something that you know will not or cannot happen, you'll be a lot less likely to lean in to something that's going to reactivate that ole amygdala. When we try to manifest our own futures, we are likely to start worrying. "What if I imagine a wedding to my current partner in great detail, and we break up in three weeks?" Or "What if I dream about buying a little bungalow across the country, but my career holds me back and I feel resentful about it for the rest of my life?" The point here isn't to try to start manifesting a future for yourself. The point is to reengage the part of your brain that dreams—boundlessly.

CHAPTER 7

Lily's Boxing Match

It's Never Too Late to Heal

The hero feels just as frightened as the coward. It's what he does that
makes him different. It's what he does that makes him a hero, and
it's what the other fellow doesn't do that makes him a coward.

Cus D'Amato

Lily is dying.

I can see gravity pulling at her, sucking her cheeks in, and
pressing her shoulders down into the earth. She is losing weight
so quickly it feels as though she is turning to sand in front of me and
slipping away into the sea.

Lily is dying, and I don't know if she knows. She has never said it. In
fact, we don't talk about her cancer at all. The doctors are busy trying
to figure out where it started, which means that it's everywhere now. I
know this, but I don't know if she knows this. She is busy trying to
unravel the giant ball of yarn that is her life. I try to remember that the
vicissitudes of her cancer are not relevant if she doesn't want them to be.
She is not here to talk with me about her cancer. She is here to talk about
her family and her horrific childhood and to learn how to finally let go
of fear. She doesn't have time to talk about cancer. Her time is running
out, and there's so much she hasn't figured out yet.

Lily is dying, and I know that she is dying, and I do not know if
she knows that she is dying. It is certainly not the first time I have been

alone with a piece of terrible knowledge that really belongs to someone else. Still, the sentence "Lily is dying" marches through my head regularly, like some sentinel standing guard and making rounds, keeping order, making sure I don't forget. Sometimes I whisper it out loud to myself just to give it somewhere else to be.

Lily wears oversized chambray shirts and sweaters to keep her warm or to hide her weight loss. One morning, as she reaches for her coffee mug and takes a sip, her giant chambray shirt sleeve slips from her wrist to her elbow and reveals her forearm. I gasp. She is skin and bones.

We have a lot of work to do, and we are running out of time.

She calls me one Friday evening, breathless. I have friends over, so I sneak into the bathroom and close the door to answer.

"Lily? Are you okay?"

"I had an epiphany," her raspy voice races to explain. "I've been mining my memory and I found a little fragment here and I think I know why I've always been so afraid. This is the piece."

I sit down on the bathroom floor, put my hand over my left ear to block out the sound of wine glasses and music coming from the other side of the door, and take a deep breath.

"Okay! Well. That's great. What is the piece? What did you find?"

"Oh!" Lily breathes as deeply as she can and keeps scratching along. "Well, after we spoke the other day, I had this memory of hiding in my closet when it was about time for my father to come home. I had decided that this time, I was not going to be waiting at the foot of the stairs like the rest of the kids. I was taking a stand. It was a very big deal to not be all shiny and perfect and standing there to wait on him. The only time that was allowed was if you were sick, and you had to be really sick to not show up."

The words sound like they are leaving raggedy knife marks in the back of her throat, but somehow Lily sounds delighted. She sounds free.

"Anyway, so I was sitting there in my closet. I had pulled the door closed and pulled my knees into my chest, and I was almost giddy at the thought of what was about to happen. I would not get up, and my father would see that I was my own person."

Lily is not usually this dynamic or enthusiastic when she talks about her past. She is usually subdued, drawn, slow going.

"I'm noticing how much of you there is in this story, Lily. Most of the time when you talk about your childhood, all of the 'you' sort of seeps out of the story in the telling."

"I know," she says. "This is the piece. I was subverting the power, flipping the table, just like you always talk about."

SUBVERTING POWER

In a famous boxing match in 1974 called "The Rumble in the Jungle," Muhammad Ali was pitted against George Foreman, and Ali was slated to lose. Foreman was the undefeated world heavyweight champion and known for the incredible force behind his punches. Ali was not just labeled the underdog; there were serious concerns that he might be killed in the ring.

Ali had a secret weapon though, a strategy he had termed the *rope-a-dope*. Leaning back against the ropes, Ali let Foreman punch him over and over again. Covering his face, he let Foreman's powerful blows land on his arms and body and be absorbed by the ropes behind him. Ali was waiting. Foreman was relentless, but he quickly started to get tired. Power punches took energy, and Ali was saving his, punching back with quick jabs only when he could hit Foreman right in the face.

As Foreman began to get visibly tired, Ali taunted him. "That all you got, George? They told me you could punch," he whispered in Foreman's ear. Frustrated, exhausted, and now embarrassed, Foreman quickly wore out.

It was time. Ali gathered all his saved-up energy, and in the eighth round, he landed a few crushing right hooks, a five-punch combo, and one last devastating left hook. Much to everyone's great surprise, Foreman was down for the count. Ali hadn't just survived; he had won.

Ali didn't get stronger or faster to prepare for the fight. He figured out how to subvert the power and use Foreman's formidable power against him.

The word *subvert* comes from the Latin *sub*, which means "from below," and *vertere*, which means "to turn." To subvert power is to come from underneath it, to turn it over from below. Think of turning over soil or flipping meaning in an argument. There's something mischievous and empowering about subversion. It requires being engaged with something that is more powerful than you, finding its weak spots, and turning it on its end. Subversion is a kind of undoing, a taking over, a taking back.

When do we turn to subversion? When something has overtaken us, held us down, put us in a cage. When we have found ourselves powerless, helpless, without recourse. When we need to take back the reins.

Lily's situation is a perfect example. Her father was one of those charming, debonair Fred Astaire types outside the house and a complete nightmare at home. From the outside, everything looked picture-perfect and pristine. Inside, the house was on fire and every person inside was slowly burning alive. Lily had gotten out in one piece—really, she was the *only* one in her family who had gotten out in one piece. Every one of her siblings had turned to drugs or alcohol to cope. Several of them were already dead.

Survival is a tricky concept though. Lily had survived in some ways and not others. Her life was functional; she had a career and a family and *some* healthy relationships. But the fear that had settled inside her bones when she was a kid being raised by a mercurial and terrifying father was still there. That fear made her decisions for her. It shaped her belief systems. It was the lens through which she saw the world. That kind of fear is silently corrosive. It makes it impossible to feel safe, to believe in anything that is good, to rest. It tears apart your relationships, leaving the people around you wondering why you don't quite believe in them, why they can't quite get to you.

When hypervigilance becomes a way of life, all you see is potential threat—nothing else. Being in any kind of relationship with someone who is driven by that kind of fear is like trying to have a deep and vulnerable conversation with a sniper on watch. You can sit there and bare your soul as much as you like, but 99 percent of his focus is in the crosshairs. As it must be.

Lily asked me once if I thought she was cold. "Do I come off that way? Cold, uninterested, incapable of vulnerability?"

"No," I said.

The truth is a bit more complicated. Whoever said this to her has gotten it partly right and partly wrong. Lily is not cold. She is very warm. She laughs easily, and when she does, it takes her over. She throws her head back and laughs with her entire body. It is contagious. She's charming, delightful, curious. And also. Lily operates from a certain remove. She is always put together in such an intentional way that some people probably feel that she is invulnerable. There is something about her that is hard to reach, probably because she lives behind a long sniper rifle and is always watching for threats.

"So I'm waiting in the closet, absolutely determined. I can feel the clock ticking seconds and minutes outside." Her voice scrapes on and starts to slow. "And then I hear the car come up the driveway, the wheels crunching and turning over gravel. And in less than a second, *without deciding*, I am down the stairs, waiting for my father just as I was supposed to. Feeling utterly betrayed by myself. All of that effort, that decisiveness, gone in less than an instant."

"I have to tell you, Lily, I know this isn't the point of the story, but I'm a little relieved that you didn't stay there in the closet. I worry about what would have happened to you if you had."

"I know," she says. "Isn't it so sad? It's so sad. But here's the thing. Since we've been talking, now I understand why. I wasn't betraying myself; I was protecting myself. That automatic response that I must flee or disconnect is what made it so that I could get out of there alive. But what I had to give up was *my own identity*. So now what? What do I do? How do I get it back? I need to get it back."

There are many differences between Lily and Ali, but the most important one is this: Ali's opponent was alive and right there in the ring with him. Lily's opponent has been dead for years and years and years. How can she fight against an opponent who exists only in her mind?

This is the beauty of subversion. It's never too late. In fact, sometimes the longer you wait, the more effective it is. We can't always subvert our opponent in the moment, the way Ali did with Foreman. Sometimes the event happens too quickly and knocks us out too fast for us to take the reins back. But it is misguided to think that just because we didn't fight back in the moment we are forever doomed. Just because you can't subvert power in the moment doesn't mean you can't subvert it at all.

TAKEAWAYS AND TOOLS

Lily is battling with a version of herself that lives in her mind. Her father told her—in his words and through his behavior—that she was not enough. That she was not acceptable. That her purpose was to appear but not exist. To quiet herself. To be perfect. She was a reflection of him, and he was an alcoholic, so her role was to be proof to the world that he was an upstanding citizen and a good father. If she was okay, that must mean that he was okay too—the classic codependent smokeshow.

The reason she doesn't have an identity—or doesn't feel like she has an identity—is because for her whole life she has been at war with the labels her father put on her. She either decided to embody them with such devotion that she would be beyond reproach (*I will be so perfect no one can ever claim otherwise!*) or decided to reject them (*I refuse to be quiet!*). Either way, she was still engaged with them, still living in a cage.

Regardless of our upbringing, most of us are at war with a version of ourselves that lives in our minds. This version is cobbled together using other people's judgments of us or fears about us. This version is made up of labels that other people slapped on us, and they stuck, usually before we were even able to realize that it was happening. Whatever this version looks like, part of its trick is to convince you that it is *all you are.*

Not enough. Unacceptable. Hard to love. Unathletic. Shy. Tomboy. Bad at math. Too much. Overly emotional. Too sensitive. Fat. A liar. Broken.

We lose our sense of identity when we engage with these labels because whether we are accepting them or rejecting them, *we are still being reduced to them.* The genius of these labels is that they trick us into thinking they define us. That they are all we are. Our unintegrated traumatic experiences do that too. They trick us into thinking that the worst things that ever happened to us are the *only* things that ever happened to us.

If Lily sits there and sorts through these labels, she doesn't feel like any of them fit quite right. She can either be unacceptable, perfect beyond reproach, or abused. She struggles against and with these labels because they are wrong *and* right. They are who she is and they are not at all who she is. She's at war.

She is calling me because she has discovered something in this memory of sitting in her closet as a kid and choosing to defy her father. Even though she didn't actually do it in the moment, the fact that she decided to reveals a capacity within her: To subvert the power that is acting against her. To pave her own path forward. To claim her own identity from those attempting to reduce her to their labels. To light up her little hope circuit.

It's easy to look at Ali's rope-a-dope and credit the method for winning the fight. But what made the discovery of the method possible was that Ali refused to be reduced to "underdog." If he had just focused on what everyone else was saying that he was—old, not as powerful as Foreman—he would have lost the fight. Instead, he accepted the fact that he was not as powerful as Foreman and moved on to *what else* he was: Able to take a punch. Brave enough to try. Ten kinds of clever. Seeing himself as something beyond the one thing everyone was trying to get him to be made it possible for Ali to create his own identity amidst all the noise. And he won.

TRAUMA TOOL: ONE HUNDRED OTHER THINGS

Simply rejecting labels is problematic for three reasons. One, the rejection still involves being engaged with the label, which sticks around and tries to reduce you as you try to defy it. If you are trying to reject the label that you are not enough, for example, *anything* you do becomes proof that you either are or are not enough. The second reason is that sometimes these labels are *so* stuck on and have been there for so long that they are impossible to get off, even with razor blades and nail polish remover. And the third reason is that sometimes the labels are true. Foreman *was* more powerful than Ali. Lily *was* abused.

The trick is to avoid the belief that the label is the *only* thing that is true. Here's an exercise that can help when certain labels start trying to convince you that they are all that you are.

Step 1: On a piece of paper, write down *every* negative label that rolls around in your head. True or not, outrageous or not—it doesn't matter. Get the labels down on paper. *Useless. Failure. Burden. Broken.* Go!

Step 2: Take a moment and notice how this list makes you feel. Do you feel tense? Sad? Frantic? Small? Does it make your stomach hurt or your palms sweat? Write that down too.

Step 3: Now, on that same piece of paper, write one hundred *other things* that you are. Yes, *one hundred.* These one hundred other things cannot be negative, but they can be *anything. You wear glasses. Love chocolate. Drink obscene amounts of coffee. Eat spaghetti squash. Have three pairs of Vans. Cannot eat fettuccine alfredo without having heartburn for two entire days.* If you can't make the list all at once, that's entirely okay. Come back and keep adding to it until you have one hundred things. *Great friend. Tall. Pretty funny. Nice eyes.*

Step 4: Take a moment and notice how this list of one hundred things makes you feel. Do you feel more at peace? Do you feel less trapped and owned by the measly list of labels now that you see them next to a list of one hundred other things that you are?

*

You want to know what happened to Lily, don't you?

As we ended our call that night, Lily had one final revelation to share.

"Oh, I almost forgot the most important thing!" she exclaims as I prepare to hang up and go back to my friends who are waiting on the other side of the bathroom door. "They figured it out! The cancer is in my liver. Isn't that the oddest thing? Both of my parents and all my siblings are alcoholics, and *I'm* the one that ended up with cancer in my liver. It just makes so much sense!"

Now I am standing in front of the bathroom sink and I have to hold onto the sides of it while Lily is talking. The room spins and I see red. I want to smash everything I can get my hands on because her bouncing, dancing voice gives away what I was worried was true. Lily doesn't understand. If the cancer is in her liver, it's everywhere. It doesn't matter where it started. It's *everywhere*.

Lily *is* dying.

In an email to her the next day, I write about a quote from Emerson that I love.

> There's this line in Emerson's essay "Experience" that I never understood, but last night it started to make sense. In the essay, he's grieving the death of his little son. He says: "I know better than to claim any completeness for my picture. I am a fragment, and this is a fragment of me." It comes at the end of the essay, when he's sort of "finishing up" his grieving process, and I knew it was significant but couldn't figure out why.
>
> I think that the last step of grieving shouldn't be called "acceptance." It's too bitter a pill to swallow. It should be called "reordering" or "perspective." There's a moment right when we think we can't take any more, when we are convinced that we are broken down, taken over, and finished— and right there in the middle of all of that despair, perspective creeps in. "I am a fragment, and this is a fragment of me." I am a tiny piece of this world. This world that has a purpose within and without me. I am just a piece of it. And these

things that happen, no matter how world-ending they seem, do not and cannot define me. They are fragments.

It seems strange, but it's comforting to me. It's comforting to think that intensity can only exist in moments. No matter how total something seems, it can never be. Everything has its own place, and time, and ending. Life-changing events are exciting, horrifying, unbelievable, and devastating, but they are temporary, finite. Life is not. Life is immense.

So what does that mean for you?

All the terrible things that have happened to you are locked in a place far away. They cannot threaten you, they will not take you down. They might appear and ask to be looked at again so that you can gain something beneficial from them, but they do not define you. They will not take you down, even if you don't have the strength to deal with them. Your upbringing, that moment in the closet, your relationship with your father are all fragments of you. And if there are some things that need to be processed, they will come up naturally and you'll deal with them in whatever way you need to. But you are still in control; you can put them down and shut them up and walk away. You are infinitely more than where you came from, than what you've lost. No matter what it feels like now, that is the truth.

And if you're sick of mining ancient history, maybe it's time to find a way to put it down. It is what it is, and it is in the past. There's no need to pick at the scab if the skin underneath is already healing. It'll fall off on its own. We don't always need to go back and pick at those things. And if we do need to go back and find out how or why the injury happened, you must do that slowly or you'll just end up bleeding all over the floor. If there's something in the past that you think needs to be looked at, take it out slowly, glance at it in pieces, and distract yourself the rest of the time. It may not feel like it, but you have control.

You are doing *so much work*. The peace will come, I promise that. And I don't promise things that I don't know for sure—ever.

This may not help at all but it's what I've been thinking, so there you go. Just be kind to yourself. You feel how you feel. If you're tired, sleep. If you are hungry, eat. If you feel like screaming, scream.

You will be better by the end of the year. I know that you will.

Notice how I didn't *promise* she'd be better by the end of the year? I never promise things I don't know for sure.

One last thing about Lily. Though her story and the conversations here are completely true, and the email is verbatim, I haven't been honest with you about who she is. Her name is not Lily, it is Suzanne. And she was my mother. She died a few months after we had this series of conversations—and just two short years after my father died.

I wanted to tell you about her because I wanted you to know there is no end to healing—and I mean that in a hopeful way, not a damning one. I wanted to show you that *it is never too late to heal*. I wanted you to know that you don't reach some arrival point and ascend to a better way of life. I wanted you to know that we heal while we are dying. Is there anything that captures the aching vicissitudes of life more perfectly than that?

I wanted you to know that if you are still working, if the work stretches on endlessly in front of you and feels like it will never be done, you are not failing. You are doing it right.

CHAPTER 8

Finding Our Way Home

A New Understanding of Trauma

> Always, love! the earth
> moves and heaven holds.

Friedrich Hölderlin

W hat is trauma? It seems like that question should be easy to answer, but as I discovered when I first waded into the subject in graduate school, it is anything but. The best definitions I could find, the ones that seemed to really grasp the nature of trauma, were those willing to straddle the abyss between metaphor and clinical symptom clusters. My favorite definition came from William James, who described it as a lasting psychological injury spurred by especially disorienting events. He said that these "psychic *traumata*" were best thought of as "thorns in the spirit, so to speak."[1] Traumatic experience is not simply an injury that leaves a bruise. Traumatic experience pierces the spirit. Like a thorn from a rose, something essential tears off from the experience and lodges itself, painfully, in the psyche, the soul.

Just like a thorn in the skin, this psychic thorn needs to be drawn out, extracted. And the wound needs to be tended to. If this extraction and tending doesn't happen, the trauma will simply remain present. It may even encyst, fester, become infected, and threaten to take over the entire system, regardless of how small it was when it first pierced your spirit.

The body responds to a thorn or a splinter by setting off an inflammatory reaction. We might not notice the splinter at first, but we will notice the inflammation, the throbbing, the skin warm to the touch, the oozing infection. Just because these symptoms are not pleasant does not mean that they are unwarranted or a sign of our brokenness. They are the opposite. The body initiates this reaction to survive. It does so because it is strong. In a similar way, the body begins a sophisticated response to thorns of the spirit. It does so in order to survive. It does so because it is strong. If we don't feel ashamed and weak when our body responds to protect us from physical thorns, then why should we feel ashamed and weak when it mounts its own response to spirit thorns?

A great societal lie claims that our response to traumatic experiences must be quick, neat, and effortless, and if it's not, we should be ashamed. This lie is harmful in many ways, but especially because too often it keeps us from reaching out to others for help. On top of that, our collective misunderstanding of the trauma response, coupled with an outdated clinical definition of trauma, means that when we do reach out, the people we turn to are often ill equipped to help or support us. Instead, their "help" is unhelpful at best and damaging at worst, reinforcing the lie that our response to trauma is a sign of our shame, our weakness, our failure.

The truth is that when we start the healing process, we are committing to a lifelong path. Along this path are moments of panic, moments of integration, moments where old memories unexpectedly pop up unbidden. Healing involves treating the memory, treating the nervous system, *and* treating the way we relate. One of the most easily accessible and beautiful ways that we heal is in therapeutic relationships with people who can help us bear what is or has become unbearable.

STARTING AFRESH: REDEFINING TRAUMA

This basic human need to reach out to others and receive help from others is reflected in a new definition of trauma proposed by Robert Stolorow, a brilliant philosopher and psychologist. He defines trauma as any experience (acute or chronic) that meets these two criteria: the emotions it brings up are (or become) unbearable, and it lacks a relational home.[2]

This definition is powerful because if you are trying to figure out whether you are struggling with trauma, all you have to do is answer one question: Was that experience (or has it become) unbearable? If you are trying to figure out how to help someone else who is struggling with trauma, it gives you a clear direction of what to do: provide a relational home. Let's unpack what each of these pieces means.

The first criterion, that trauma is unbearably emotional, solves the problem of what counts as traumatic without stretching the word *trauma* to meaninglessness. Unbearable is quite a high bar, one that likely cannot be met by a store not having pumpkin spice lattes or a professor handing out a challenging chemistry exam. It is also a bar that allows the person going through the event to determine what was unbearable to *them*.

Just because we have survived something does not mean that it was bearable. When something is bearable, it means we have done two things: seen through the initial emotions *and* folded it into the larger story of our life. We have felt the feelings and integrated the memory. When something is unbearable, it doesn't mean we did not survive it; it means that we either could not see through the initial emotions or could not successfully fold it into the larger story of our life—or both. Because this process doesn't always happen instantaneously, we might not even know that something is unbearable until years later when it shows up as a behavior, or as a pattern that keeps appearing in our relationships and getting in the way of our lives.

This second criterion, that trauma lacks a relational home, helps us understand both what can be so shattering about overwhelming experiences and what we can do when we or someone close to us is suffering. To understand what a relational home is, consider first the meaning of the word *home*. The Indo-European root of the word is *tkei*, meaning "to settle, to dwell." In order for our life experiences to become coherent memories that we can refer to and recognize as things that are in the past, rather than things that are happening right now, they need to settle. They need somewhere to dwell.

When our experiences are mundane or easy to understand and sort through, they can find their way to a dwelling place in our memories relatively easily. Our brain files the memories in an organized way. When they are unbearable, we will need help. We need help as our brain wrangles with the disorganized, fragmented memories it had so hastily stuffed away during the original overwhelm. We need help as we examine the disruptive meaning tags that were slapped onto those memory files. So we turn to other people who have been through similar experiences to help us understand what they mean for us, what their dwelling place in our lives and memories might be. If you've ever asked a friend how they made sense of their divorce while going through your own, you were asking for a relational home. If you've ever validated someone's overwhelm by saying, "Ouch, I've been there too," you've provided a relational home. When we cannot do that—because we cannot bring ourselves to speak about what happened, because we cannot fully remember it, or because the people we reach for dismiss us—what was initially unbearable becomes lastingly so.

In fact, finding a dwelling place for our experiences is critical to the functioning of our nervous system. As we saw in chapters 2 through 7, when something unbearable becomes lastingly so, we remain chronically stressed, chronically overwhelmed, and chronically dysregulated.

At this point, you might be wondering about the specific calculus of the relational home. How do I find one? Do I need one right away, or will it be just as powerful if I find it years down the road? Do I just need one relational home? If I find it, can I stop going to therapy?

Sometimes you find a relational home by seeking out a therapist. Sometimes you find one completely by accident. It's great if you can find one right away, but sometimes a relational home is even more powerful if you find it later. It's almost never a one-and-done deal. The aftereffects of a traumatic experience are a bit like shrapnel: you find shards years later in unexpected places. One relational home heals one shard, and another heals a different shard.

The point is that there are no hard-and-fast rules. This might seem frustrating, but I think there's magic to it. The first-grade teacher who reminds you every day that you belong can counter the fact that you feel like your only job at home is to be invisible. After feeling completely trapped in your last relationship, the partner who lets you be the one to pick what music you listen to at dinner can make you feel free. When you feel like you have been let down or abandoned by every person in your life, the bus driver who always shows up at the exact expected time, and with a huge smile on her face, can remind you that reliability does, in fact, exist. One of the things that makes us so wildly vulnerable is the fact that we are *both* harmed and healed through relationship. Just as someone's thoughtless words can invoke years of hot-faced shame, someone else's kind gesture can undo years of feeling utterly unseen. The truth is, we *all* hold the keys to someone else's relational home.

Just because we need a therapeutic relationship in which to find our relational home doesn't mean the only person qualified to talk about trauma is a clinical therapist. As you may remember from chapter 1, clinical psychology still has a long way to go in repairing its broken understanding of trauma. All the lies, half-truths, and misinformation that permeate society still lurk in many professional therapists' offices too.

A few years ago, my marriage started to splinter and shatter. I was stunned by the intensity of this loss. I had recently moved, and so I needed to find a new therapist to help with this loss. In our third or fourth appointment, I sat on the couch and started to chronicle a bit more of my disbelief at what was happening. My therapist, a cowboy-looking older man, stopped me mid-sentence and then paused dramatically, leaning back into his chair for effect.

"It's always the same shit with you, isn't it?"

I blinked for a moment, absolutely stunned. Then I picked up my bag and stood up.

"Well. I think we're done here, sir."

He started to speak again—about how I was shutting down and that this wasn't going to help my process. I put my hand up and just kept walking. I wasn't even fully down the hallway before I started looking for another relational home. By the time I had gotten into the elevator, I had texted a friend about what this "therapist" had said. This time, I found a dwelling place. By the time I got into my car, I was laughing— partly to release the absurdity of what had just happened and partly in great relief for the therapists I had encountered *before* this man. I still shudder to think what would have happened if he had been my therapist when I was seventeen and trying to cope with a sexual assault. Or six months after the shocking and sudden death of my father, when panic attacks were grabbing me by the throat with such relentless force that I wondered if ending my own life was the only way to stop them. If I had met him then and he had told me I was full of shit, I would have believed him—100 percent.

He was, by the way, not some two-bit therapist. He had degrees in both psychotherapy and psychiatry and a PhD from Harvard, and he had completed his residency at one of the most acclaimed psychiatric hospitals in the United States. I had chosen him carefully after days of due diligence. I tell you this because I want you to know that several degrees and many years of experience does not guarantee that someone is prepared to offer you the relational home you need. Sometimes it's the friend you text from the elevator. The larger point is this: it is dangerous to assume that the only person who can provide a dwelling place for your unbearable experience is a certified clinician. First, sometimes that certification *does not* guarantee a safe place. Second, when we believe that the only place trauma healing can occur is in a therapist's office, we miss how very powerful and healing *we all are for each other*, all the time.

Any relationship that can provide you with a relational home, a place where you can get help bearing what is unbearable, is a therapeutic one. A therapeutic relationship is simply an alliance. The members (therapist and patient, coach and client, boss and employee, friend and friend) ally themselves to one another in the interest of a common goal. To intervene therapeutically is to attend to, the way we might attend to a wound, or a garden. The word *attend* comes from the Latin *atendere*, which literally means "to stretch toward." What a beautiful idea! That we might stretch toward one another in our isolation and pain. That we could unite ourselves toward the defeat of an obstacle or simply toward growth. That we might imagine our lives as gardens and learn how to attend to them. That together we can dig our fingers into the cold soil, pull out any weeds that threaten to overtake the space, and carefully choose and plant new seeds.

I have worked extensively with two populations I have almost nothing in common with: combat veterans and previously incarcerated gang members. With members of both populations I acted in my capacity as a life coach who specialized in trauma and was there to help them reintegrate into society. Sometimes we talked about the future but mostly about the present—the very present, the just-this-morning present. They would tell me about the way the present can get completely and suddenly eclipsed by the past. I would do all I could: I validated, demystified, and gave them tools. We would make plans and troubleshoot and check back in with tiny wins and big ole stumbles.

What I did not expect to hear as often as I did was this: "You get it, MC. You. Get. It."

Hearing these words always stunned me. On the face of it, I absolutely *do not* get it. I do not have any life experience that helps me understand what it is like to be born into a family of gang members and recruited into a gang at the age of seven. I do not have any life experience that helps me understand what it is like to be summarily dismissed from career military service because you are struggling with crippling anxiety after four tours in Iraq. I think what they were really saying was this: "You attune to me. We are allies. You stop here and stand with me in front of this overgrown garden. When I am feeling overwhelmed, you help me find where the weeds are. You stretch to help me pull them. We tend together, and we grow."

What I realized was that I don't have to have lived it to "get it." Shared experience is *not* what lays the foundation for a relational home. Attunement is. Which means that any of us can get better at knowing how to attune to someone. Any of us can learn to find which pieces of an experience are especially overwhelming. We can learn how to point out these pieces and ask, if we are able, whether we might hold them for a little while, like a colicky baby, so the other person can get a break.

✳

As I was writing this book, I got an email from a concerned researcher. He had come across a quote of mine in a *National Geographic* article and was worried about my work. He wanted to let me know that recent studies have shown traumatic brain injury (TBI) to be the real source of any traumatic symptom, and that my time to talk about the way that trauma impacts our lives outside of physiological explanations was running out. He was wrong about the first part: not all psychological traumas can be sourced to TBIs. But I worry he was right about the second part: that time is running out to advocate for a new understanding of trauma.

In chapter 1, we talked about the phases of the history of the study of trauma. As we stand in this new phase, I find myself having both a nightmare and a dream.

My nightmare is this: We continue down the path of misunderstanding trauma. We lean in to all the things we are getting wrong—that trauma is a sign of weakness, that it is so prevalent it is trivial, that triggers are a sign we have been hardwired to self-destruct. We keep drawing dividing lines that push any discussion of trauma into dark and secret places. Instead of correcting our course, we again return trauma to anathema, recreating the chaotic cycle of intense study before turning away from it. We send those who are struggling back into the darkness and sweep everything we've learned under any rug we can find so that next time, when we are forced to realize that trauma does not go away and we do need to face it, we can't even reach for what we've already learned. My research, teaching, work with clients, and this book are my ways of keeping that nightmare at bay.

My dream is that we take this current phase of increased awareness about trauma and use it to build a solid foundation for understanding and coping with trauma. That we reframe the discussion of trauma entirely. That we start correctly understanding trauma as unbearable emotional experience that lacks a relational home. That this understanding becomes so common it's known to all of us, from tweens to seniors. That we learn to look at trauma from a variety of disciplines rather than just one. That we sort out the science from what history has hijacked. That we get our heads straight and realize that the trauma response is a neurobiological adaptation rooted in strength. That the trauma response is simply the way our biology responds to overwhelm. That we have control over this response and can reverse much of the damage it can cause when it doesn't turn off. That we stop shaming ourselves for the coping mechanisms that we reach for in survival mode. That we take seriously the role of providing a relational home to whomever we have capacity to provide it for.

Tiny Little Joys

joy was his song and joy so pure
a heart of star by him could steer
and pure so now and now so yes
the wrists of twilight would rejoice

e. e. cummings

I want you to come away from this book with six things. Five of them I've already talked about.

The first is the knowledge that whatever you are struggling with, you are not alone.

The second is the understanding that our responses to traumatic experiences are automatic and protective, and they are indicative of our inner strength, not a sign of weakness or disorder.

The third is the grace to forgive ourselves for whatever we reached for out of desperation and overwhelm. We can't heal if we don't put down the shame.

The fourth is the awareness that we can rewire our brains and invite our nervous systems to have experiences of safety and connection even if we've spent our whole lives feeling unsafe and disconnected.

The fifth is a better understanding of the way that we can heal—and heal each other—by learning how to recognize and provide a relational home for what is unbearable.

The sixth has to do with joy—tiny little joys.

I think sometimes we misunderstand the scale of things. We assume that great big problems require great big solutions, that when sadness looms large, our happiness must grow equal in size to counter it. These assumptions are wrong.

Joy is an anchor—heavy, solid, reliable. It sinks to the ocean floor and tethers us so we are not unmoored but can only wander so far. From the boat, all we can see is the anchor cable, which looks small and insignificant in comparison to the wide sea. But its scale doesn't matter. It doesn't need to be as wide as the sea to anchor us.

When I finally returned to my apartment in New York City after my father died, I would often find myself lying flat on my back on the floor, letting waves of grief crash over me. I was sure I would drown, that my heart would shatter, that the world would stop. There was nothing but these waves, this sorrow, that ache. But slowly—and always—the world would start filtering back in, and I would notice some tiny, lovely thing around me. The way the light was spilling across the floor in diagonal rainbows. The way the soft, looped pastel rug felt underneath my fingers. A breeze winding around the curtains in front of my giant windows. The blue of a vase from across the room. Laughter from the street. A tiny pang of hunger in my belly. A memory of something that made me *almost* laugh.

None of these things brought my father back or woke me up from my terrible dream. They didn't eradicate my anxiety or speed up the grieving process. They didn't solve anything. But they did anchor me. They pulled me back in, made sure I didn't wander too far. They reminded me that although trauma may feel like an ocean of ceaseless pain, joy—absurd, audacious, outrageous—keeps on existing right there alongside it. All we have to do is let it in.

I haven't told you much about my father, only about the loss of him. This makes sense because this is a book about trauma and his sudden death changed the entire trajectory of my universe. But having him as my dad is what set the universe in motion in the first place.

The first loss I ever suffered was that of my stuffed bunny, aptly named, well, Bunny. My family had gone to visit my older brother at college and stayed in a hotel. I left Bunny underneath my pillow and forgot her there. At the time, I'd had Bunny for so long and loved her so intensely that the only person on earth who could recognize her as a bunny was me. Her eyes and ears had been loved completely away. The music box that lived inside her little torso had stopped playing long, long ago. Most of her cotton stuffing had come out, leaving her deflated. She had been white at one time, but her fur had been loved off to the backing, and what remained was a dingy yellow color. So we can't really blame the hotel staff for not recognizing that Bunny was a bunny, let alone a cherished friend and confidante. I left her behind, and they threw her away.

I was eight and I was *bereft*.

The most difficult time of the day was bedtime. Getting to sleep without the comfort of the bunny that I had lived my eight years with was quite a task. I would put on my pajamas, get into bed, and listen to a story. Twenty minutes later, I would get out of bed and go downstairs with tears spilling down my face. My stomach hurt. I couldn't sleep. How could she really be gone? Would I ever love anything like that ever again? Are you supposed to replace a missing bunny with a new one? Or was that disrespectful? (I was an intense kid.)

My dad, who had six children and a full-time dental practice, who had likely just read me the story to put me to sleep, and who was enjoying what was probably his first free moment to himself since he got up at six that morning, would stop whatever he was doing and sit with me. He would pour a couple of ounces of ginger ale into two rocks glasses, and we'd sit side by side at the kitchen table as if it were some smoky bar in the Bronx. We would just sit with it all—the enormity of the loss, what it meant to my little world, and the seriousness of the questions this loss brought up. We discussed options. If I were to get a new bunny, what kind of bunny would it be? A replica of the old bunny? Or something entirely new? Sometimes we just sat in silence, sipping ginger ale.

He never judged me, never told me to stop crying, never told me that I should be over it by now. He never said it was silly to be this sad or I should be ashamed of my intense little heart. He just sat with me.

I distinctly remember realizing that if I made a decision about what kind of bunny I should have next (if any), it would mean moving on. And moving on would mean no more late-night ginger-ale bar chats with my dad.

Sometimes people ask me how I spend so much time in the dark—thinking, researching, and talking about trauma all day every day. I usually have cheeky answers to this question, but I think it's because the dark doesn't scare me. It never really has. Because the first time I was plunged into it, my dad taught me that you don't go to war with it. You don't push it away. You don't let it swallow you.

You just sit with it.

Preferably right next to someone you trust, someone who shares your reverence for the enormity of it, someone who will pour you a rocks glass full of ginger ale and never tell you it's time to get over it, someone who will gently remind you that horror is not all there is to life. Someone who will keep the door open for you to notice the tiny little joys—like the tingly feeling of ginger ale bubbles bursting against the roof of your mouth. Someone whose very presence *is* a tiny little joy.

Acknowledgments

This book would not have been possible without my agent, Laura Yorke, who I believe took me on as a client primarily because when I first wrote to her, I identified as "an academic gone rogue." Thank you, Laura, for being so infinitely reassuring during this process. Thank you to Jennifer Brown at Sounds True, who wore a straw hat to our pitch meeting, which instantly put me at ease, and who saw the promise in this project before it had much promise to see. Thank you to Amy Rost for editing this book like a fairy godmother might—tiptoeing around with a magic wand and making my words sing. Thank you to the editorial team at Sounds True for catching all the things I would never have caught, and for making sure that the book hits all the right notes and none of the wrong ones.

Thank you to Colin David Whyte, who answered approximately five hundred messages that started with, "Hey, what's that word that means . . ."; who consistently reminded me that a metaphor is more effective if it makes sense; and who gave meticulous notes on the first draft of this manuscript, writing comments like, "I mean . . . you sound like kind of an ass here, not sure if that's intentional?" Bird by bird.

Thank you to John Kim, who has been so effortlessly influential in my life that it's getting a little bit ridiculous. I have completely lost track of who I might be without you, John. Thank you to my clients, whose fearlessness humbles me daily. Thank you to my students, who regularly restore my faith in the future of humanity. Thank you to Chris Rhoden for always, *always* getting it, and for being the person to whom I can send a text that simply says, "sneaky duck, so fine!"

Thank you to the trauma llamas, who kept me company and kept me laughing for the pandemic years and beyond (I hope). Thank you to Lisa, Jake, Luke, Matt, and Dan for being as excited about this as Dad would have been.

And thank you to Mark Griffin for helping me recover my glittering little soul amidst all the wreckage, for the conversation in a weird bar in Boulder that planted the seed that would become this book, for the clam bowl, and, well, for everything else. Some things just can't be captured in a list.

Notes

Introduction: We Are Not Broken

Opening quote: Jalal al-Din Rumi, "There's Nothing Ahead," *The Essential Rumi*, trans. Coleman Barks (New York: HarperCollins, 1995), 205.

Chapter 1: Repairing Our Understanding of Trauma

Opening quote: Leslie Jamison, *The Empathy Exams: Essays* (Minneapolis: Graywolf Press, 2014), 5.

1. Abram Kardiner and Herbert Spiegel, *War Stress and Neurotic Illness* (New York: Paul B. Hoeber, 1947), 1.

2. Judith Herman, *Trauma and Recovery: The Aftermath of Violence—from Domestic Abuse to Political Terror* (New York: Basic Books, 1999), 7.

3. David J. Morris, *The Evil Hours: A Biography of Post-Traumatic Stress Disorder* (New York: First Mariner Books, 2016), 13–14.

4. Herman, *Trauma and Recovery*, 7.

Chapter 2: Malcolm's Fight Club

Opening quote: Tim O'Brien, *The Things They Carried* (New York: Mariner Books, 2009), 36.

1. American Psychiatric Association, *Diagnostic and Statistical Manual of Mental Disorders*, 3rd ed. (Washington, DC: American Psychiatric Association Press, 1980), 236–238.

Chapter 3: Gabe's Broken Heart

Opening quote: Maurice Merleau-Ponty, "Eye and Mind," *The Primacy of Perception: And Other Essays on Phenomenological Psychology, the Philosophy of Art, History, and Politics*, ed. James Edie, trans. Carleton Dallery (Evanston, IL: Northwestern University Press, 1964), 162.

1. Sigmund Freud and Josef Breuer, *Studies on Hysteria*, trans. James Strachey et al. (New York: Basic Books, 2000), 35.

2. Abram Kardiner, *Traumatic Neuroses of War* (Mansfield, CT: Martino Publishing, 2012), 227.

3. Kardiner, *Traumatic Neuroses of War*, 223. Italics added for emphasis.

4. David J. Morris, *The Evil Hours: A Biography of Post-Traumatic Stress Disorder* (New York: First Mariner Books, 2016), 41.

Chapter 4: Grace's Referred Pain

Opening quote: Emily Dickinson, "Pain—has an Element of Blank—," *The Complete Poems of Emily Dickinson*, ed. Thomas H. Johnson (Boston: Back Bay Books, 1976), 323.

1. American Psychiatric Association, *Diagnostic and Statistical Manual of Mental Disorders*, 3rd ed., revised (Washington, DC: American Psychiatric Association Press, 1987), 238.

2. Oisin Butler et al., "Trauma, Treatment and Tetris: Video Gaming Increases Hippocampal Volume in Male Patients with Combat-Related Posttraumatic Stress Disorder," *Journal of Psychiatry and Neuroscience* 45, no. 4 (July 2020): 279–287; Antonia Brühl et al., "Preventive Efforts in the Aftermath of Analogue Trauma: The Effects of Tetris and Exercise on Intrusive Images," *Journal of Behavior Therapy and Experimental Psychiatry* 64, no. 4 (September 2019): 31–35; Muriel A. Hagenaars et al., "Tetris and Word Games Lead to Fewer Intrusive Memories When Applied Several Days After Analogue Trauma," *European Journal of Psychotraumatology* 8, no. 1 (2017): doi.org/10.1080 /20008198.2017.1386959; L. Iyadurai et al., "Preventing Intrusive Memories After Trauma Via a Brief Intervention Involving Tetris Computer Game Play in the Emergency Department: A Proof-of-Concept Randomized Controlled Trial," *Molecular Psychiatry* 23, no. 3 (March 2018): 674–682.

Chapter 5: Max's Hourglass

Opening quote: Dietrich Bonhoeffer, *Letters and Papers from Prison*, 3rd English ed., ed. Eberhard Bethge, trans. Reginald Fuller et al., additional material by John Bowden (New York: Touchstone, 1997), 176.

1. Ralph Waldo Emerson, *Essays and Lectures* (New York: Viking Press, 1983), 471.

2. Ralph Waldo Emerson, *Journals of Ralph Waldo Emerson: With Annotations* (New York: Reprint Services Corporation, 1911), 150.

3. Emerson, *Journals of Ralph Waldo Emerson*, 157.

4. Emerson, *Journals of Ralph Waldo Emerson*, 151.

5. Emerson, *Essays and Lectures*, 473.

6. Leslie Jamison, *The Empathy Exams: Essays* (Minneapolis: Graywolf Press, 2014), 5.

7. Jacques Derrida, *The Work of Mourning*, trans. Pascale-Anne Brault and Michael Naas (Chicago: University of Chicago Press, 2001), 107.

Chapter 6: Erica's Trauma Bond

Opening quote: *Northern Exposure*, season 3, episode 5, "Jules et Noel," directed by James Hayman, written by Joshua Brand, John Flasey, and Stuart Stevens, aired October 28, 1991, on CBS.

1. Donald G. Dutton and Susan Lee Painter, "Traumatic Bonding: The Development of Emotional Attachments in Battered Women and Other Relationships of Intermittent Abuse," *Victimology: An International Journal* 6, no. 1 (January 1981): 146–147.

2. Sigmund Freud, "Beyond the Pleasure Principle," *The Standard Edition of the Complete Psychological Works of Sigmund Freud*, trans. James Strachey et al. (London: The Hogarth Press and the Institute of Psychoanalysis, 1955), 12–13.

3. Freud, *The Standard Edition of the Complete Psychological Works of Sigmund Freud*, 18.

4. Freud, *The Standard Edition of the Complete Psychological Works of Sigmund Freud*, 23.

5. Freud, *The Standard Edition of the Complete Psychological Works of Sigmund Freud*, 21.

6. Christopher Ricks, responding to Galen Strawson's lecture, "We Live Beyond Any Tale That We Happen to Enact," April 11,

2010, Boston University, wbur.org/worldofideas/2010/04/11/we
-live-beyond-any-tale-that-we-happen-to-enact.

7. Bessel van der Kolk, *The Body Keeps the Score: Brain, Mind, and Body in the Healing of Trauma* (New York: Penguin, 2015), 32.

Chapter 7: Lily's Boxing Match

Opening quote: Cus D'Amato, "The Coward and the Hero Feel the Same," *Against the Ropes*, December 29, 2015, youtube.com/watch?v=1nwkTN1zFt4.

Chapter 8: Finding Our Way Home

Opening quote: Friedrich Hölderlin, as quoted by Martin Heidegger, *Poetry, Language, Thought*, trans. Albert Hofstadter (New York: Harper and Row, 1971), 223.

1. William James, "Hysteria," *Psychological Review* 1, no. 1 (1894): 199.

2. Robert Stolorow, *Trauma and Human Existence: Autobiographical, Psychoanalytic, and Philosophical Reflections* (New York: Routledge, 2015).

Epilogue: Tiny Little Joys

Opening quote: e. e. cummings, "my father moved through dooms of love," *E. E. Cummings: Complete Poems (1913–1962)* (New York: Harcourt Brace Jovanovich, 1972), 520–522.

Recommended Resources

Chapter 1: Repairing Our Understanding of Trauma

Judith Herman, *Trauma and Recovery: The Aftermath of Violence—from Domestic Abuse to Political Terror* (New York: Basic Books, 1999). This book is considered canon in the history of the study of trauma. Herman is a clinical psychologist, and she writes powerfully about the similarities between seemingly disparate kinds of trauma. It's a great place to start if you're interested in the history of the study of trauma or the topics of domestic violence and political terror.

Bessel van der Kolk, *The Body Keeps the Score: Brain, Mind, and Body in the Healing of Trauma* (New York: Penguin, 2015). If you're interested in the science of trauma, this book is a great pick. Van der Kolk is a clinical psychiatrist and researcher and one of the world's leading trauma experts. He wrote this book to help trauma survivors and those who support them understand how trauma impacts the body as well as the mind and how to facilitate healing.

Chapter 2: Malcolm's Fight Club

Jonathan Shay, *Achilles in Vietnam: Combat Trauma and the Undoing of Character* (New York: Simon & Schuster, 1995). Shay is the psychologist who coined the term *moral injury* in his work with Vietnam veterans. In this book, he draws parallels between the soldiers in Homer's *Iliad* with Vietnam veterans struggling with PTSD.

Nancy Sherman, *Afterwar: Healing the Moral Wounds of Our Soldiers* (New York: Oxford University Press, 2015). Sherman, a philosopher and ethicist, builds significantly on Jonathan Shay's work. In this book, she explores the kinds of combat injuries that are not accounted for in psychology or medicine: those that shatter one's sense of morality.

David J. Morris, *Evil Hours: A Biography of Post-Traumatic Stress Disorder* (New York: First Mariner Books, 2016). Morris, a war journalist who struggled with PTSD after returning home from Iraq in 2011, writes beautifully about his experience. He explores the history of combat trauma and considers some of the more problematic treatment methods in current use.

Chapter 3: Gabe's Broken Heart

Michael White and David Epston, *Narrative Means to Therapeutic Ends* (New York: W. W. Norton, 1990). White and Epston begin with the recognition that sometimes our stories lock us in, failing to represent us or our lived experience. They then explain, using examples from their own practices, how "restorying" can play a critical role in healing.

Arthur W. Frank, *The Wounded Storyteller: Body, Illness, and Ethics, 2nd ed.* (Chicago: University of Chicago Press, 2013). Frank is a medical sociologist who specializes in the way that those who suffer from illness tend to be reduced to their status as wounded. He argues that this reductionism is problematic, as people are more than their illnesses and diagnoses. Using the stories of those who have struggled with illness, Frank shows the way that the story can transform and reveal the wounded.

Peter A. Levine, *Healing Trauma: A Pioneering Program for Restoring the Wisdom of Your Body* (Boulder, CO: Sounds True, 2008). Levine is the creator of Somatic Experiencing therapy, a modality that begins with the assumption that in order to heal from trauma, we must work with the way that trauma gets imprinted on the body. In this quick little book, you get a snapshot of Levine's program and lots of exercises to try.

Stanley Rosenberg, *Accessing the Healing Power of the Vagus Nerve: Self-Help Exercises for Anxiety, Depression, Trauma, and Autism* (Berkeley, CA: North Atlantic Books, 2017). If the sections in this book on the vagus nerve piqued your interest, pick up Rosenberg's book next. Rosenberg seamlessly weaves together complicated science with practical techniques to increase vagal tone and lower anxiety.

Chapter 4: Grace's Referred Pain

Jennifer Sweeton, *The Trauma Treatment Toolbox: 165 Brain-Changing Tips, Tools & Handouts to Move Therapy Forward* (Eau Claire, WI: PESI Publishing, 2019). This super handy guide offers a brain-based approach to healing from trauma. Sweeton includes helpful diagrams and descriptions of the brain structures active in the trauma response alongside practical and easy tools that you can practice. This book is meant to be used in conjunction with therapy and is a great addition to the healing process.

Robert D. Stolorow, *Trauma and Human Existence: Autobiographical, Psychoanalytic, and Philosophical Reflections* (New York: Routledge, 2015). Stolorow holds dual PhDs in philosophy and psychology and has also had some stunning personal experiences with trauma. In this book, he considers the ways that trauma is central to human existence, rather than an experience that lies outside the norm.

Chapter 5: Max's Hourglass

Mary-Frances O'Connor, *The Grieving Brain: The Surprising Science of How We Learn from Love and Loss* (New York: HarperOne, 2022). O'Connor is a neuroscientist who has spent her career studying the way that grief impacts the brain. In this groundbreaking book, she unpacks her neuroimaging research, explains what it tells us about grief and the brain, and offers practical advice about how to navigate the grieving process.

Florence Williams, *Heartbreak: A Personal and Scientific Journey* (New York: W. W. Norton, 2022). When Williams went through a shattering divorce, she turned her journalist's mind on her own experience to figure out why the loss was wreaking such havoc on her body. Merging science, alternative therapies, and her own life story, this book gives a gripping account of grief and healing.

Chapter 6: Erica's Trauma Bond

Emily Nagoski and Amelia Nagoski, *Burnout: The Secret to Unlocking the Stress Cycle* (New York: Random House, 2020). This book provides a close-up look at the stress response system—especially for women. Though this book isn't specifically about trauma, what works for stress also applies to trauma because they both operate on the same responses in the body. The Nagoski sisters do an incredible job demystifying the stress response system, and the book is chock-full of tips and tricks for managing daily stressors.

Dan Tomasulo, *Learned Hopefulness: The Power of Positivity to Overcome Depression* (Oakland, CA: New Harbinger Publications, 2020). This is a completely unique book in the field of positive psychology. Tomasulo guides you out of hopelessness with compassion, evidence-based practices, and practical advice.

Chapter 7: Lily's Boxing Match

David Kessler, *Finding Meaning: The Sixth Stage of Grief* (New York: Scribner, 2020). Kessler is a grief researcher who worked closely with Elisabeth Kübler-Ross on her research on the five stages of dying. In this book, Kessler corrects some of the misunderstandings about how these stages work and discusses how finding meaning can be a part of grief that enables you to reframe the loss entirely. This work should be essential reading for anyone who is suffering through loss.

Resmaa Menakem, *My Grandmother's Hands: Racialized Trauma and the Pathway to Mending Our Hearts and Bodies* (Las Vegas: Central Recovery Press, 2017). If you are interested in the way that trauma uniquely impacts the lives of folks in the Black, Indigenous, and People of Color (BIPOC) community, this book is a great place to start. Menakem considers some of the ways that racism in America creates trauma and how that trauma becomes embodied. He considers pathways to healing that are based in both cognitive and somatic work. Beyond this, it's just a beautiful read.

Mark Wolynn, *It Didn't Start With You: How Inherited Family Trauma Shapes Who We Are and How to End the Cycle* (New York: Penguin, 2016). If you're interested in the burgeoning field of epigenetics, which looks at the ways that the effects of stress and trauma can be transmitted genetically through generations, pick up Wolynn's book. You won't get bogged down in confusing genetic terminology. Wolynn unpacks how family trauma can take hold, how to recognize when it has, and what to do about it.

About the Author

MaryCatherine (MC) McDonald, PhD, is a research professor and life coach who specializes in the psychology and philosophy of trauma. She has been researching, lecturing, and publishing on the neuroscience, psychology, and lived experience of trauma since beginning her doctorate in 2009. Her work focuses on thinking critically about how we understand, define, and heal from traumatic experience. She is passionate about destigmatizing trauma and mental health issues in general, as well as reframing our understanding of trauma in order to better understand and treat it.

After receiving her master's degree at The New School, where she researched traumatic loss and mourning from both philosophical and psychological perspectives, she went on to complete her PhD at Boston University. She has published several research articles and book chapters, as well as two books on trauma, *Merleau-Ponty* and *a Phenomenology of PTSD: The Hidden Ghosts of Traumatic Memory* and *American* and *NATO Veteran Reintegration: The Trauma of Social Isolation and Cultural Chasms.*

In addition to her academic work, McDonald has a thriving life-coaching business. She has coached individual clients and corporate employees since 2010 and created trauma-based curriculum for non-profit organizations in New York, Virginia, and California that serve previously incarcerated individuals and veterans.

About Sounds True

Sounds True is a multimedia publisher whose mission is to inspire and support personal transformation and spiritual awakening. Founded in 1985 and located in Boulder, Colorado, we work with many of the leading spiritual teachers, thinkers, healers, and visionary artists of our time. We strive with every title to preserve the essential "living wisdom" of the author or artist. It is our goal to create products that not only provide information to a reader or listener but also embody the quality of a wisdom transmission.

For those seeking genuine transformation, Sounds True is your trusted partner. At SoundsTrue.com you will find a wealth of free resources to support your journey, including exclusive weekly audio interviews, free downloads, interactive learning tools, and other special savings on all our titles.

To learn more, please visit SoundsTrue.com/freegifts or call us toll-free at 800.333.9185.